Performing Consumers

D1585437

Performing Consumers is a searching exploration of the way in which brands insinuate themselves into the lives of ordinary people who encounter them at branded superstores.

Looking at our performative desire to "try on" otherness, Maurya Wickstrom employs five American brandscapes to serve as case studies: Ralph Lauren; Niketown; American Girl Place; Disney store and *The Lion King*; and the Forum Shops at Caesar's Palace in Las Vegas. In this post-product era, each builds for the performer/consumer an intensely pleasurable, somatic experience of merging into the brand and reappearing as the brand, or the brand's fictional meanings.

To understand this embodiment as the way that capital is producing subjectivity as an aspect of itself, Maurya casts a wide net, drawing on:

- the history of capital's relationship with theatre,
- political developments in the United States, and
- recent work in political science, philosophy, and performance studies.

An adventurous study of theatrical indeterminacy and material culture, *Performing Consumers* brilliantly takes corporate culture to task.

Maurya Wickstrom is Assistant Professor of Drama at the College of Staten Island, City University of New York. Her work has appeared in leading journals, including *Modern Drama* and *Theatre Journal*, and in a new anthology on Disney.

Performing Consumers

Global capital and its theatrical seductions

Maurya Wickstrom

 Routledge
Taylor & Francis Group

NEW YORK AND LONDON

First published 2006
by Routledge
270 Madison Avenue, New York, NY 10016

Simultaneously published in the UK
by Routledge
2 Park Square, Milton Park, Abingdon, Oxon OX14 4RN

Routledge is an imprint of the Taylor & Francis Group, an informa business

© 2006 Maurya Wickstrom

Typeset in Baskerville and Gill Sans by
Florence Production Ltd, Stoodleigh, Devon

Printed and bound in Great Britain by
TJ International Ltd, Padstow, Cornwall

British Library Cataloguing in Publication Data
A catalogue record for this book is available from the British Library

Library of Congress Cataloging in Publication Data
Wickstrom, Maurya.
   Performing consumers: global capital and its theatrical seductions/
   Maurya Wickstrom.
      p. cm.
   Includes bibliographical references and index.
 1. Stores, Retail – Psychological aspects.   2. Marketing.
 3. Merchandising.   4. Consumer behavior.   5. Brand name products.
 6. Themed environments.   I. Title.
   HF5429.W514 2006
   658.8'342–dc22   2006000390

ISBN10: 0–415–33944–8 (hbk)
ISBN10: 0–415–33945–6 (pbk)
ISBN10: 0–203–44904–5 (ebk)

ISBN13: 978–0–415–33944–5 (hbk)
ISBN13: 978–0–415–33945–2 (pbk)
ISBN13: 978–0–203–44904–2 (ebk)

For Erin and Naoise
roots and wings

Contents

Acknowledgments

My deepest thanks to all of you: Jill Dolan, my brilliant mentor, living and working minute by minute to bring a better world into being; it was my great good fortune to find you. Jennifer Parker-Starbuck and Josh Abrams, generous friends, to whom I owe so much. Sandy Fluck, amazing editor, lifelong friend, fiery progressive, and to Dick for being, always, our friend. At Routledge, Talia Rodgers and Minh Ha Duong, for making this possible. My early teacher, Jack Amariglio, who took me up into the world of left ideas, and whose passion for them held me there. My teacher Marvin Carlson, whose erudition and steady belief in me have mattered so much. Ramón Rivera-Servera, for laughs, encouragement, and stimulation. My students Young James Kenny, Michelle Philippin, Victoria Venezia, and Andrea Batista, whose creativity, intelligence, and kindness kept me buoyed up during challenging times. Allison, Kate, Liz, and Laura for the lifelines. Gordon and Betty Wickstrom, who taught me from the cradle how much both politics and theatre matter. My daughter Erin and my son Naoise, into whose wise hands I am glad some of the responsibility for the world to be will fall. And, finally, Joel, real companion, dancing till the day is done.

Also, thanks to the following publications and the editors, Loren Kruger, Nathan Stucky, and Mike Budd, who worked with me on this material in other versions. The chapter included here, "*The Lion King*, mimesis, and Disney's magical capitalism," is developed from two other published essays: Maurya Wickstrom (1999) "Commodities Mimesis, and *The Lion King*," *Theatre Journal*, 51(3): 285–98, © The Johns Hopkins University Press, reprinted with permission of The Johns Hopkins University Press, and "*The Lion King*, Mimesis and Disney's Magical Capitalism," in Mike Budd and Max H. Kirsch (eds) (2005) *Rethinking Disney: Private Control, Public Dimensions*, The Wesleyan University Press. The chapter, "Robots, gods and greed: the theatrum mundi in the Forum Shops at Caesar's Palace," was developed from Maurya Wickstrom (2001) "In the Body of the Commodity We Shall Triumph over Ruin: Performance at the Forum Shops, Las Vegas," *Theatre Annual: A Journal of Performance Studies*, 54 (Fall): 63–94, © College of William and Mary.

Introduction

> The blessing that the market does not enquire after one's birth
> is paid for by the barterer, in that he models the potentialities
> that are his by birth on the production of the commodities that
> can be bought in the market.
>
> (Horkheimer and Adorno 1972: 12)

In 1995 the Disney Corporation opened its first New York store.
One dark, rainy afternoon I traveled to its inauspicious location
in the Staten Island mall. I was a Disney novice, unexposed, even
as a child, to its vast inventory of products. Not knowing what I
would find, I knew only that I hoped to discover here some means
of critical attention. I hoped to find a way to see how corporations
so successfully yoke us, and our children, to themselves.

The store was overwhelming, immersive – dense in imagery,
reference, fields of light. Most striking was that everything in the
store's design and the products it displayed promised our "magical"
transformation into something other than ourselves. Over our
heads, Donald Duck as cinematographer was filming us, and, as
the film rolled out, we appeared not as ourselves but as Minnie,
Mickie and Dumbo. Toy and costume packaging promised that
we would be "living as" or "experiencing just like" Simba or
Pocahontas. It became clear that Disney was at work evoking the
theatrical pleasures of corporeal translation, saturating the store
with this suggestion that we should want "to be" Disney characters. I watched two adult women in the girls' costume section. One
woman took a pink Little Mermaid nightgown and held it out all
along her body. She smoothed it against herself and thrust forward
one hip in a pose intended to be alluring. Her face transfused with

light. For an instant, at least, she had what she seemed to long for. She became, bodily, other than herself, more part of Disney's world than her own.

What I saw as I began to visit other branded retail environments echoed what I saw at Disney and became the central thesis of this book: corporations produce subjectivity as aspects of their brands through mimetic and identificatory processes akin to those of performance, somatic and embodied. They reach into our corporeal desire to be like others, to take on shapes and forms unlike one's own.

Because this corporate reach is so somatic, the brick and mortar of the store is essential as the site of our performance. Store designers overtly poach in the theatrical. They have deemphasized the consumption of specific commodities and instead create experiential environments through which the consumer comes to embody the resonances of the brand as feelings, sensations, and even memories. As if we were actors in the theatre, as consumers in branded spaces we loan the brand's character the phenomenological resources of our bodies. We play out its fictions, making them appear in three dimensions, as if they were real. Embodied, the story the brand is telling feels real.

At the same time, we know very well that the story is made up. It seems that moving on a spectrum between the made up and the real is an important source of pleasure in postmodern culture. Our consumption practices are shaped by our theatrical ability to hold the real and the not real as a simultaneous instance of embodied experience, an ability to live the truth of the make-believe. Michael Taussig names what we experience with a phrase I'll use often in the book, "the really made up" (Taussig 1993: 86).

The leader of a fake "boy band" 2gether, Kevin Farley, provides an insightful account of the really made up: 2gether was originally formed with the intention to parody boy bands like 'N Sync and Backstreet Boys. The five members of the band, including 35-year-old Kevin Farley, who describes himself as overweight and bald, approached MTV with their "mockumentary," in which they sang satirical songs. In a completely unexpected turn of events, they became overnight sensations. Teenage girls went as crazy for 2gether as they did for 'N Sync, even though they were completely aware that 2gether was not a "real" boy band. In his radio report on the band, Robert Siegel comments that, "Some of the press coverage of 2gether has portrayed the band's teen-age fans as hapless, hopeless victims, adolescents too unsophisticated to distinguish what's real from what's fake" (Siegel 2000: 4). However, he continues: "Mark and Brian Gunn prefer to see it another way. They view the fan's embrace of 2gether not as evidence of the teenager's lack of sophistication, but rather as a signal that they are in fact more highly evolved consumers" (Siegel 2000: 4). Farley says:

> What's interesting to me is that people watch so many shows right now that plug themselves as reality shows and yet, also people know that they're engineered in countless ways. And people are able to hold within themselves something being an artifice and something being real at the same time. And in many ways 2gether is a lot like pro wrestling. All the fans completely know that it's fake and yet they give themselves over to it wholeheartedly. And what's interesting to me is that in some ways now, you have to admit of the form. You have to show both the artifice and what motivates the artifice. And I think, actually, I give credit to people not for mistaking the construct, but for admitting of the construct and being able to indulge in it at the same time.
>
> (Siegel 2000: 4)

In brandscapes, the shopping/entertainment environments that have for so many of us become an organizing feature of our life experience, we "admit of the construct" but indulge it at the same time. We know that buying and consuming branded products will change little in lives we most likely wish could be different. We know the sensorial riches of the stores serve the brand's inventions. But we nevertheless flock to them, desiring the pleasure of materializing the brand's transformative promise as if it were our own.

The Coke store in Las Vegas, for instance, is a tall, green, translucent building in the shape of a Coca-Cola bottle. Once through the doors, it is we who fill it, as if we ourselves were coke. We circulate up and down through the many floors of the store, liquid, contained by the inner walls of the bottle, the hollow body of the brand. Our identity is meant to be brought close to, or be indistinguishable from, the brand. In one part of the store, there is a recreation of a soda fountain from the 1950s. Given a hint of costume in a soda jerk's paper hat, we are encouraged to fashion ourselves within, or as, an invented Coke moment. We are American citizens from the 1950s, happy and carefree because of our association with Coke, our indispensable place in its circulation. In another area there's an in-store theatre where ordinary people's experiences with Coke, their "Coke stories," are presented on film. We are invited to write down and submit our own. There is a chance that our stories will be chosen to be enacted, that our life will be materialized as a Coke life, taking on all the vibrancy of Coke. Elsewhere, we can drink from a fountain, from whose hundreds of spigots different flavors of Coke from all over the world spurt forth. While drinking the Coke it is impossible to avoid thinking of the fountain of life because "Coke is life." I take in Coke as bodily substance. I feel like I am shimmering with all that a Coke America and a Coke world means, a place that "is life."

The brand becomes a full-body costume that opens itself for us to crawl inside. Our legs stretch into the leg openings, arms into arms, head into head. We cause it to move, as we move inside. As it moves, we discover that the costume skin is translucent; we can see through it to the lights of a different world, the world the product inhabits, the world we get to play as if we were now in.

Although most of us would describe our experience in these stores as recreation, it is in fact a form of labor that is coming to be one of the dominant, compelling, actions of our lives. We labor such that the imaginative core of our beings is indentured to the brand, so pleasurably that we'd never think to resist. This is what the corporations are banking on. This is the core of what I describe in the course of this book. This is the threat to, dare I say, our humanity, about which we should become passionately aware. I watch the children around me drowning in it. Two of my chapters center on corporations which specifically target the young. Disney has always aimed its seductions at children, but, increasingly, children are being identified as the last frontier for marketing and product sales by other corporations. And so, each mindful moment of the child, the trajectory of imaginative life, is seized by an ad, a Game Boy, an iPod imported movie (with product placements). And, of course, adults join in with their own branded clothes, cars, and pastimes. It's hard to remember, or imagine, alternative ways of being. The corporations have turned us into affective, embodied, theatrical laborers on their own behalf. This, I believe, is a form of the immaterial labor that Michael Hardt and Antonio Negri say will become the dominant form of labor in the emergent stateless capitalism they call Empire. This labor is immaterial in terms of its product, not necessarily in its means of production. It creates affect, social relations, networks. Our corporeal work in the stores is a significant piece in the emergence of an apparatus that supercedes all prior forms of sovereignty and smoothes the way for the "realization of the world market" (Hardt and Negri 2000: xiii). The name I've given to this theatrical kind of immaterial labor is corporate performance.

Performance

Performance is a widely used term. Used as the core of a cultural analysis, it can be applied to varied activities including, but not restricted to, artistic production like theatre.[1] It has also been used as a rubric under which it is possible to suggest theories about representation that diverge from those perceived to adhere in the traditional theatre. Theatre is often thought to rely on an apparent correlation between the representation and a real original of which it is, supposedly, the faithful copy. Performance, on the other hand, can refer to cultural production that is independent of an authentic, original model, and of any obligation to a written text. By performance, then, we are afforded a broad conceptual scope by which we may mean any in a wide range of practices, occurring in many different places, and without depending on imitation. By using the term performance in the book, rather than theatre, I am deliberately positioning my work within this field. It allows me to move outside the boundaries of the theatre into the more quotidian environment of the store, and, in particular, into the five retail spaces that I write about here: Ralph Lauren, Niketown, Disney, the Forum Shops at Caesar's Palace, and American Girl Place.

At the same time, I want to make sure that theatre and performance, if not exactly synonymous in this book, work conceptually alongside one another. I depend for my argument on a specifically theatrical, human capacity that is often overlooked in both preferences for and critiques of realist representation. I refer here to theatre's stubborn way of slipping out from under the thumb of the real into identifications, or the abandonment of the experience of an original, real self into an experience of sameness with another. As Elin Diamond (1997: 106) says, this slip which is identification undoes the stable subject, the true identity, which supposedly underlies representation. Another way to understand identification is as mimesis, which Walter Benjamin called our "compulsion" to "become and behave like something else" (Benjamin 1978: 333).

Understood mimetically, rather than representationally, the theatre is able to exceed the boundaries of the real. Through the sheer force of our embodied identifications, our mimetic aptitude, we can create a made up real which calls into question the veracity of any determining original. We can play in a strange doubleness, creating something that is not real but feels as if it were. Mimetic theatricality moves us onto that spectrum of the really made up. I rely, as the deep content of my definition of performance, on this mimetic content of the theatrical, which has little to do with truthful imitation, and everything to do with the productive capacities of embodiment and the protean self.

In 1944, Theodor Adorno and Max Horkheimer, two of the first theorists of mass culture and consumer society, argued that the Enlightenment and its cultural and political legacy have meant that humans have lost their mimetic affinities. Like Benjamin, they thought of mimesis as a sensual kinship between forms. They too were interested in it as a tactile, corporeal apprehension of otherness. But since the Enlightenment, they thought, our relationship to the world (including objects, nature, other people, and even our own selves) is, by contrast, one of estrangement. In their analysis, we objectify nature, objects, and ourselves as we seek the domination over them that will allow us manipulate them to our advantage in a market-driven world. Contemporary corporate culture, however, seems to belie Adorno and Horkheimer's claims. Although propelled irrevocably by the Enlightenment, it has recalled mimesis as a key strategy to bind us to itself. Mimesis becomes, paradoxically, a means to domination. The otherness toward which the performer/consumer whom I theorize in these pages is drawn is, as I've suggested, none other than the brand and its meanings, the shape, or "character" scripted for us by the commodity form.

Historical precedents

In this book I am concerned primarily with contemporary environments where the strategic use of mimesis that I've described is reaching its full-blown, postmodern form. Nevertheless, it is important to know that capitalism and performance have been bound up in one another since the inception of capitalist economic structures in the early modern period.

In that perplexing time, in a new and emerging market, new forms of circulation, of goods and people, became requisite. Subjectivity was reconfigured as the performance of multiple selves: selves made up in response to a market which was causing old meanings, old moorings, including those anchoring subjectivity, to be uprooted. During this period, the very meaning of the term "market" changed. Instead of a geographically established place it became instead a "process" (Agnew 1986: 41) in which exchange value made its historical appearance as a "perceived . . . property of the commodity distinct from and alien to its specifically useful or aesthetic aspects as a human artifact" (Agnew 1986: 42). Disengaged thus from use-value the commodity was rendered into the abstractness of the money form, distributed by traveling tradesmen. This new placelessness, this fluid market, was lived by the thousands of people uprooted from their tenantries, and from the marketplace in which they had previously met face to face to exchange the goods they had produced. During this period about one-third of England's land was privatized, and those unable to buy or rent joined a growing itinerant population, people who had only their labor power to sell. They entered the market as "a range of different identities . . . composed of dispersed, serial 'selves'" (Fumerton 2000: 218).

The period was full of literature developing this concept of self. There were, for instance, advice books to which literate people could turn for help in creating "a self composed . . . of . . . successive performances" (Agnew 1986: 83). Francis Bacon worked at a theory of how people might exceed the limitations of their original natures to bring forth a second, or artificial nature. He thought that character and character traits might be thought of as investments, in the double sense the word had at the time: as both a garment and a commercial asset yielding profit. Like an investment, the character might be stitched together, and changed, an investment whose value would change according to the fluctuations of the market.

The professional actor, whose trade was made possible by the new capitalist market, was a central figure, both metaphorical and literal, through which anxieties about successful performances of marketable identity could be articulated and negotiated. Thomas Hobbes, defining his "artificial person," wrote that he is the same thing as an actor on a stage. The poet John Hall wrote: "Man in business is but a Theatrical person" (Agnew 1986: 97). Playwrights observed, recorded and theorized this person. For instance, in their play *If It Be Not Good, the Devil Is In It* (1610–12), Dekker and Webster include the following speech, claiming that in the precarious new world ruled by the commodity the only security lies in one's hoard of selves.

> That, for which many their Religion,
> Most men their Faith, all change their honesty,
> Profit, (that gilded god) Commodity,
> He that would grow damn'd rich, yet live secure,
> Must keep a case of faces.
>
> (Agnew 1986: 57)

And on the public stages, audiences watched the actor as a literal instantiation of the new person. No longer the guild member, the temporary performer of the medieval pageants whose identity was rooted as the baker or the weaver, this actor was someone who seemed to have no identity other than the serial ones of the stage. The actor modeled for the audience the possibility that identity is not natural, but made, performed into existence.

From this moment capitalism embarked on a long process of unfixing the subject from any mooring, from any underlying truth, and encouraging the subject to make appearances, or enactments, as valences of the commodity. At every step this process has entailed the use of the theatre and/or performance as a laboratory, a model, or a favored mode of expression.

Although a full study of the imbrication of capital and theatre would be a book in its own right, I have included amidst my contemporary account some brief glimpses backward. These "historical echoes" are set in boxes to indicate that they are not essential to the chapter in which they're included. My readers may skip them, if they choose to do so, without losing its sense. Taken together, they are very far from establishing anything like a comprehensive survey of the ways that capital and performance have been mutually productive. They are, rather, small and discontinuous narratives, meant to evoke the history that ghosts our own mimetic relations with brand culture, to keep it in our sidelong vision. We are, let us remember then, a hybrid constitution of commodity, brand, and human that has its precedent since even before this scene John Wheeler described in 1601, a couple hundred years after people began to "fashion" themselves in the multiple shapes favored in the market.

> All the world choppeth and changeth, runneth and raveth after Mars, Markets and Merchandising, so that all things come into Commerce, and pass into traffic in all times, and in all places: not only that which nature brings forth but further also, this man maketh merchandise of the works of his own hands, this man of another man's labor, one selleth words, another maketh traffic of the skins and blood of other men, yea there are some found so subtle and cunning merchants, that they persuade and induce men to suffer themselves to be bought and sold.
>
> (Bruster 1992: 41)

Guides for reading

My reader should be forewarned that the details of the stores I've written about here are enormously time bound, precisely because the market has to be infinitely adaptable and its enactments fluid. By the time you are reading this, store themes, specific displays, even whole stores, may have been dismantled, liquidated, or changed. By 2004, for instance, Disney's branded superstores had fallen into disrepair. Although as of spring 2005 Disney reversed plans to sell its European retail stores – for lack of buyer interest – it's sold its North American retail outlets to the clothing store, A Children's Place. However, my time-bound examples are used to analyze more general processes that are necessary to the ongoing health of corporate culture and are not, in their general outline, transitory. It is my hope that these examples will be useful to my reader as a focusing lens to begin to see other examples in your own time and place.

The perspective I offer here is restricted to the American scene, and, though I suspect that branded superstores in other major Western cities are similar to those I describe, I cannot make that claim from first-hand experience. Nor can I make a claim that my theorizations of the brandscapes I study here are based on any kind of ethnographic work. I've not gathered evidence, and there is nothing empirical about my findings. My intention, rather, is to offer imaginative, critical, and theoretical engagements with these spaces through my own embodied experience – trusting that in so doing I am making an accurate account of at least some of the allure of these spaces, and of the damage they do. Finally, each chapter is a separate case study of a retail space, complete in and of itself. A reader can, if you prefer, choose to read only one or two of the studies. The reader who does move through the book consecutively will encounter some repetition of ideas that are fundamental to my analysis of several of the spaces, although at each site those ideas are developed and applied slightly differently. The chapters have been ordered for cumulative effect and understanding, leading up to the most insidious example of corporate performance, American Girl Place.

Moving on from here

Sadly, our generally pleasurable and willing immersion in corporate performance indicates to me that the optimism about resistant practices within consumption itself – inaugurated by DeCerteau and blossoming in the discipline of Cultural Studies – is no longer justified. Nor is it any longer possible to champion, with much conviction at least, the view that the deconstructed, fluid self is an alternative to power in that it dismantles essentialized subject positions. That it may do, but it is also the self that performs capital's faces. As Hardt and Negri say, "The ideology of the world market has always been the anti-foundational and anti-essentialist discourse par excellence" (Hardt and Negri 2000: 150). Nor is it politically useful to go on proposing, as some still do, that the body must be spoken of as an effect of discursive production. Those who hold this position think that to speak of it otherwise, as a material thing, is to trade in dangerous essentialist categories, and to make unfounded claims for the validity of presence. If we wish to understand or intervene in the astonishing consolidation of corporate power in the past few years, we need to look for fresh perspectives.

Many progressive scholars have already moved forward into new kinds of analyses of the structures of power. Some argue that it is time to move on, carrying the gains of poststructuralism with us, into critical, theoretical, and political risk taking: considering again questions "of a universal (Alain Badiou 2003), or of Judith Butler's "'common' corporeal vulnerability" (Butler 2004: 42), or of the human and of the body as the grounds for a universal commonality (Terry Eagleton 2003), or of the sensate body as the location for change (Brian Massumi 2002). The reclamation of the body as a material thing seems necessary when it is not hard to see that the right, unlike the left, never lost sight of the possibilities for manipulating the body. Massumi, whose work on affect is sourced in the sensual organization of the kinesthetic body, says that, "In North America at least, the far right is far more attuned to the imagistic potential of the postmodern body than the established left and has exploited that advantage for at least the last two decades" (Massumi 2002: 44).

The materiality of the body is also important to Hardt and Negri's analysis of contemporary power. Their arguments, along with Massumi's, are important for Chapter 1. A "new theory of subjectivity" (Hardt and Negri 2000: 129) is necessary, they say, to correctly analyze production and reproduction in Empire. This new theory must include the body since, "the productivity of the corporeal, the somatic, is an extremely important element in the contemporary networks of biopolitical production" (Hardt and Negri 2000: 30).

By biopolitical power Hardt and Negri mean a form of power that reaches into the entirety of social life, all of which becomes a place of production. In the disciplinary form of power Empire replaces, institutions imposed their control on individuals from above or outside those individuals and were often met with resistance. In the "society of control" (Hardt and Negri 2000: 23), by contrast, power sinks into the entire organism and consciousness of the individual so that she herself participates actively in its reproduction: "Power can achieve an effective command over the entire life of the population only when it becomes an integral, vital function that every individual embraces and reactivates of his or her own accord" (Hardt and Negri 2000: 24).

Jon McKenzie (2001), whose work I look at quite closely in Chapter 4, takes off from the proposal that disciplinary society has been displaced by a society of control. He pushes further and claims that it is performance itself that is the organizing, structuring mode of power through which we willingly labor to make ourselves appear according to its (highly changeable) criteria. It is performance, across all social fields and researched in many diverse disciplines, that will enable us, in this emerging moment of global corporate power, to *be*. It is fairly certain that this form of being is not a state that we should desire, for it's a manifestation of the biopolitical reach of power that drives us "toward a state of autonomous alienation from the sense of life and the desire for creativity" (Hardt and Negri 2000: 23).

My work in these chapters is inspired, informed, or directly founded on these ideas. I hope I can contribute to them a sense of what is lost to us by our bodily circulation in the market, against which we seem to put up less and less resistance. The shopping experience is an aspect of conjoined effects of a corporate culture, a society of control, which all together have resulted in the decline of democracy, of political dissent, and in public helplessness in the face of the rise to power of men who are in flagrant violation of democratic processes, and the human right to well-being.

My hope is that our "sense of life and desire for creativity" will find some small space inside both individual bodies and the social body in which to germinate. Perhaps we can find a way to "perfume" our days with a hint of the recuperation of human singularity.[2] How can we become incommensurate, resisting the fundamental problem of our circulation as that abstract homogenization which is our face as the brand? How can we escape this "unity of a count" (Badiou 2003: 10)? Perhaps the body can at least be imagined again as the common ground of vulnerable humans, open to otherness, so that we have an alternative, if only imaginatively, to our experience of it as the materialization of brands. I wish to know how can we walk amidst these stores, navigate the branding, unable to immunize ourselves against their pleasures, but able to affirm in ourselves, and especially in the children of this culture, that this need not be all there is. This book is my way of naming what threatens us, and looking for a different way of seeing.

Chapter 1

On the move at Niketown and Ralph Lauren

The flagship store, built around a single brand, is an innovation of the late 1980s and 1990s, a response, in part, to a crisis in consumer attitudes. Corporations found that the falsehoods of commodity culture were becoming transparent to consumers. People were getting savvy to the fact that the commodity wasn't making good on its promises. The mere purchase of a piece of lingerie, a car, or a sports shoe wasn't delivering a sexier self, a more chic self, or a more athletic self. Corporations were challenged to find a change of address to the consumer. Nike, for instance, developed ads characterized by an ironic attitude that would separate it, in consumer's minds, from the vapid promises of prior advertising campaigns. It was to be a company with a conscience. In a Nike TV ad from this period, basketball star Charles Barkley says, referring to the shoes he wears: "They won't make you rich like me. They won't make you rebound like me. They definitely won't make you handsome like me. It'll only make you have shoes like me" (Goldman and Papson 1996: 90). The approach worked. In the course of its phenomenal growth, Nike has shaped itself so that it seems not so much a merchandiser as a soul that we can share in, inspiring us to take leave of our limitations and climb to our own personal heights.

Other corporations were also developing an image of themselves as a mystique, an essence, a set of compelling life philosophies: in other words, they produced themselves in the form of a brand. Further, the flagship store, often called entertainment retail, was initiated as the ideal medium through which the brand essence could be felt and experienced. The stores were designed to communicate the inner architecture of the brand's meanings, opening the brand to the senses (and embodiment) of consumers.

Importantly, each store was "an immersing retail environment to tell a brand's story" (Dorris 1997: 103), over and above any attempt to actually move product. When the first Niketown opened in Portland, Oregon in 1991, only half of the space was devoted to merchandise display. People weren't in these stores to buy products. They were there to experience the brand. They were there to experience the brand's essence, inspiration and soul.

Since the early 1990s, entertainment retail has become a wildly successful form of experience, ubiquitous particularly in big cities and tourist destinations. Teams of marketing experts, brand gurus, architects, theatre designers, and corporate executives are continually honing the form and intention of this brand experience to suit the evolving requirements of corporate growth and consolidation. The focus of this chapter is on two of the earliest flagships, both in New York City: Niketown, on 57th Street, and Ralph Lauren on Madison Avenue.

Immaterial labor and the brandscape

Architectural journalist Otto Riewoldt uses the term "brandscape" (instead of entertainment retail) to describe stores intended to "get the customer to identify with the world of the brand, creating a brand awareness and providing it with a deep-set emotional anchor" (Riewoldt 2002: 10). John Hoke, the Global Creative Director of Nike Brand Design, provides another, related angle on this emotional anchoring when he says that: "The Nike brand or brand experience is based on sowing the seed of a memory in your customer's mind, so that you can draw on that memory again – 'harvest' it – weeks, months, years or even decades later" (Riewoldt 2002: 103). For these men, the emotional life of the "customer" is targeted as a place of production, a deep field for the invention of memories, associations and affinities. Here the brand can be shaped, evolved, and manifested, its post-production value extracted or reaped by the corporation when the time is right.

This kind of productive labor by the performer/consumer in the brandscape corresponds to what Michael Hardt and Antonio Negri call "immaterial labor". Immaterial labor, though it may be bodily, produces the immaterial products so increasingly indispensable to postmodern capitalism: information, communication, ideas, and emotional responses. A form of labor that can be and is conducted outside any of the traditional temporal or spatial organization of traditional labor, it corresponds to the spread of postmodern capitalism's "global networks of production and control" (Hardt and Negri 2000: 58).

Most importantly, immaterial labor is "biopolitical" (Hardt and Negri 2004: 109) in that it doesn't just produce goods and services, but social life itself. Labor moves far outside of the constrictions of the industrial mode of production such that the power of capital is extended into political, cultural, and social areas of life, the boundaries between which are increasingly blurred. Immaterial laborers, who may be working at innumerable kinds of social sites, are freed from the linear and hierarchical model of the factory and assembly line. The capitalist no longer has to mandate and oversee how, when, and where labor is organized to ensure its cooperation, but rather value is "capture[d]". (Hardt and Negri 2004: 113) from the cooperative labor of workers who have organized their own creative energies. What this means is that, increasingly, the emergent form of biopolitical capitalism depends upon our cooperative, "productive capacity" (Hardt and Negri 2000: 213),[1] which is exercised across the social terrain. Hardt and Negri say that:

> Labor and value have become biopolitical in the sense that living and producing tend to be indistinguishable. In so far as life tends to be completely invested by acts of production and reproduction, social life itself becomes a productive machine.
> (Hardt and Negri 2004: 148)

Brandscapes like Niketown and Ralph Lauren are aspects of this "productive machine." The Nike and Ralph Lauren companies are dependent upon our active, creative, productive capacity as the source of their power and revenue as they traverse the globe through virtual networks of what Tran Vinh calls the "money web" (Chung et al. 2001: 434). This condition of our common social life raises for me a series of questions that are guideposts for this chapter. What characterizes our immaterial labor in brandscapes? What do we do, or feel, as we work? What exactly does our work produce? What precisely is the value to corporations that is reaped from the seeds sown deep into our productive, creative capacity? And finally, how does our productive capacity, as it is nurtured in these stores, become a capacity that is productive across brands, across corporate cultures, a revenue shared in common by all of them?

Being hit and making it up: the productive capacity of the mimetic body

In what follows, I weave in and out of my experience at Niketown, moving from its heart-stopping rhythms to the theory that might help me understand what I am doing here, and what use Nike hopes to make of me.

When I walk through the front doors into the chrome and glass futurism of Niketown, I'm awed by the power of a circular atrium that heads straight up five stories high. It's ringed by the floors of the store that open out on to it, floors boundaried by steel railings and cables, beautiful industrial engineering. It's as if I've stepped into a kind of machine, like a spaceship to elsewhere, or a transformer that might whirl me into a centrifugally engineered otherness. There are steel and chrome girders, giant columns with openings for lights that look like X-ray machines. The whole place looks and feels, in fact, like something of a cross between a futuristic fantasy and a kind of medical environment in which inexplicable machinery of the highest technological caliber promises interpretations, regenerations, or transformations of the body.

I'm caught off guard when, with a sudden swoosh, so loud it seems to vibrate from inside me, the room darkens, and, like a giant automata, a two and a half story projection screen rolls itself relentlessly downward, spilling into the heart of the atrium to the beat of pulsing techno pop. On the screen there are montages of athletes in exertions that seem superhuman, other than human, grand, beautiful, and heroic. The screen event is clearly the techno-heart of the store, pumping its blood on a rhythmic schedule.

The effect of this filmic event is overwhelming, irresistible, immediately *inside* all my senses. Walter Benjamin speculated early in the twentieth century that the new motion picture camera was a mimetic machine that inaugurated a welcome resurgence of mimesis in a modern, post-Enlightenment world from which it had been eliminated. He compared the camera to the work of the surgeon, who dissolves the distance between himself and what he perceives as his hands move deeply into contact with the organs inside the patient's body (see Benjamin 1968: 233). Michael Taussig, developing Benjamin's idea, says of this experience: "You

don't so much see as be hit" (Taussig 1993: 30). This is my sensation as the screen pours down. My heart begins to pound, my
blood begins to pump, my muscles to throb. I watch, but at the
same time, I feel myself moving, and moving as if the rhythms of
the screen were my own. I'm not moving like the athletes on the
screen. I'm not an athlete and, after all, I'm standing in one place.
But I feel beginning to explode in me a new potential to move as
if I were them, as if I were coming unfixed, unstuck, moving from
one state to another – moving as an athlete, and, maybe, moving
from my place in life.

I wonder at the awesome corporeality at the heart of this store's
design. Nike wants my body sucked into this rhythm, even as global
capital seems to rely increasingly on the incorporeal, on digital
and electronic transmission and accumulation, on the disembod-
iment of cyberspace. I'm struck by what Riewoldt (2002) calls

> the paradoxical phenomena that, by enabling and anchoring
> immediate brand experiences, the IT age has actually
> upgraded the physical location. We are not talking here about
> virtual non-experiences in the no-mans-land of the Internet,
> but about concrete encounters in real locations, where the
> world of the brand is staged and enacted.
>
> (Riewoldt 2002: 8)

It's clear that brandscape architects and designers find neither
the privilege traditionally accorded to sight and vision in the
Western world, or the seductions of the Internet, primarily useful
in seeding the brand into customers. They're working in a different
medium: it's a somatic epistemology, an embodied comprehen-
sion. They're creating mimetic environments in which there is a
"palpable, sensuous connection between the very body of the
perceiver and the perceived" (Taussig 1993: 21). Hoke, the Nike
brand designer, says:

> Our customers experience Niketown live – an immediacy that
> accounts for much of the success of this particular concept
> . . . The general public has a sense that they want more – they
> want a story, they want emotions, they want to react very
> strongly, both physically and emotionally . . . In the past, the
> tools we had at our disposal were largely non-emotive
> ones. With today's technologies – encompassing lighting, smell,

sound and vision – we are definitely able to pinpoint emotions in each customer . . . when we are designing a new store we make sure that the design takes all the senses into account. We try to create a design that is visually spectacular, and to seduce our customers with fragrances that conjure up particular emotions: we also design our products to be attractive in tactile terms, through the materials we use. To create a total experience you have to involve all the senses. In the culture we have grown up with, our understanding of the world is a highly visual one, increasingly restricted to two-dimensional forms of expression based on a computer or a television screen. Part of our work is to convey a real experience of the world, not a virtual one.

(Riewoldt 2002: 107–9)

When the driving rhythm of the techno screen and the movement of the athletes slams into me, Nike becomes a percept: it is known to me through my senses. Hoke and other brandscape architects are counting on my mimetic faculty, which can be characterized as a compulsion or desire to take what I perceive into the physiology of my own body. When Hoke talks about sowing the seeds of Nike in customers this is why he needs the body to do it, this is why he needs the immediacy unavailable through Internet shopping. Virtual shopping remains a spectral activity, the distance or difference between myself and the merchandise or brand I see there intact. If, on the other hand, I take Nike in through the physiological responsiveness of my body, the distance is dissolved. Nike is the surgeon's hands inside me, rearranging me.

There I stand, vibrating with the pulverizing, contagious experience of the swoosh, alive with a sense of how I might be changed. I begin to look around, and I notice then that I'm standing on a glass-covered opening in the floor. Looking through it, I see that about three feet below where I stand there's an old gym floor and an abandoned, battered basketball – preserved relics. Gathered toward the future, I am standing on a window to the past. Looking up and to the right, I see that there is a break in the wall of the store that exposes, behind it, what must be the wall of the old gym whose floor I've just glimpsed. The wall is encrusted with the markers of an old game, poised to begin. There are the old kind of clocks, with bulbs that can be made to light up in the shape of any number to keep time, to keep score. From this perspective, I see that the walls of the Nike store are offset from old brick walls all around. They're braced apart from them by black beams in a display of engineering which suddenly makes the store appear to me as a techno bubble suspended within an archaic athletic environment. I move toward the old wall but find that I can only get about eight feet away from it. The store floor across which I move abruptly ends at that point, revealing beneath me, again, that old gym floor.

I'm protected from the drop, the difference between my techno environment and this abandoned, aged site, by guardrails. This viewing position is touristic, archeological, like being on the brink of a dig. The excavation is without smell or flavor, without the seductions of memory that tempt us toward a movement of recovery, a journey backward toward the past (nostalgia) (see Seremetakis 1994: 4). The past I witness from the railings is only a checkpoint by which to mark my point of departure into Nike. I can't smell the past, hear it, or touch it. Without these sensory cues, there is no danger of a return.

At the same time, though, this glimpse of the past suggests that memory is something that I can invent. I reach into the past before me for my memory of a sweated body belonging to me in a time long before this. The techno wrap that's making my heart pound converges with a memory I am in the process of inventing. The convergence calls up in me the physical capacities of youth, the heart pounding, sweating, pain-mixed euphoria of being at a physical peak. The evocation of this physiologically experienced sensation – that I can in this moment believe belonged to myself when I was young (and therefore physically capable of such things) – helps me to feel as if I really could become, move, lose my constrictions like the athletes on that screen.

In feeling this moment of an invented past (and other moments yet to come), I am experiencing an aspect of the mimetic faculty; I am "sutur[ing] the real to the really made up" (Taussig 1993: 86). Mimesis is a capacity that allows us to travel a spectrum along which we encounter, or live, the truth of the make-believe. We bring invention into facticity, and vice versa. This means that I can live the made up of my Nike past and future, my Nike body, as if it were real. The invented is not *just* the made up. It's the "really made up," implying that the made up takes on, in our mimetic bodies, the qualities of the real, even as it's simultaneously imaginary.

To play this way, between the real and the really made up, is to play at a moment where what we are is not yet determined, where one thing but also another paradoxical thing might be true simultaneously. Our mimetic proclivity to play across this spectrum of indeterminacy, to take as real what is not real, is simultaneously a desire to respond to the world with "an ineffable plasticity" (Taussig 1993: 34). The self loses its boundaries; I take on the heart rhythms of the Nike athlete. The brandscape designers choose explicitly theatrical language to express their investment in this active, productive playing of otherness. Riewoldt says:

> The customer becomes an actor. With the same professional care as in a theatre, each step of each scene is carefully defined, from the props to the stage directions, transforming the sale of goods into an exciting plot in which the potential customer is not so much a passive spectator as a character in the play.
> (Riewoldt 2002: 10)

My initial mimetic response is enough to begin to understand something about how my productive capacity is triggered at Niketown, and what it might be productive of; I'm unsettled into a delicious indeterminacy, simultaneously bodily and immaterial, vaguely associated with futural and technological possibility, and shimmering with the rich potential of the chance to be other than myself. Calling out from us our mimetic tendencies as a productive capacity allows the designers of these environments to release the self from its boundaries, and to give us the sensation that our identity is escaping foreclosure (even as the script of the play reencloses us, giddy with our felt escape, into the corporate agenda). Without knowing, and here is the first hint of what my labor produces, I begin to rehearse and produce as a quality of my own subjectivity the continual, restless movement of capital. Indeterminacy and motion feel like a part of me. It feels good. My body opens and responds.

I want to bear with me into my future-becoming a fullness of being birthed in the past of that old gym. I have a heart-throbbing longing to run, to achieve that long jump, that smash of racket on ball, to give over to the abandon of the body at the limits of its beautiful abilities. The skeletal ruin of the gym recalls the power of the youthful body, the one from the invented past, but gives over the motion, the becoming of that body to Nike, where I become more attached to what I imagine, and imagine kinesthetically (I feel myself making that jump in my heart pounding, adrenalin rushing body), than to what ever really was. I'm someone in movement, on the move.

Indeterminacy and release: affect as productive capacity

Mimesis creates an ineffable yet embodied space of traversal, and in this it can be linked as a productive capacity to what Brian Massumi (2002) calls "affect". Mimesis and affect are conjoined processes in what I experience at Niketown.

For Massumi, affect is not another word for emotions or feelings. Emotions, in fact, are affect trapped.[2] Affect is a kind of pregnant fullness, an instant, always just passed, elusive, where we feel our potential, unstructured into any known form. Consciousness tends to cracks down on affect in a backward movement, recognizing it just after the fact of its occurrence. In this moment, consciousness organizes and captures affect into the form of emotions, or other kinds of situated perceptions. But affect remains as the after-image, the life-giving awareness of something that escaped, of something that will always escape, that is more than the smallness of recognizable emotion. Affect is that thing that keeps moving out from under us. It's a field of potential emergence. It's the fleeting sense that there is something about us that is not so fixed as all the gridded coordinates of our lives, including our predictable emotions, would indicate. Affect, and its escape, "is nothing less than the *perception of one's own vitality*, one's sense of aliveness, of changeability, (often signified as 'freedom')" (Massumi 2002: 36). At Niketown, in the mimctic slam of the swoosh into my body, I feel my vitality, just passed, just moving on, and it unsettles me from my fixed position. This is what Nike makes me feel. Not emotion, but affect – liveliness, movement. I'm getting ready to feel myself as a person unbound from all the coordinates that constrain me.

I move back to the center of the atrium. The film event is over. The screen pulls itself up and the store's general lighting is restored. I see what I'd not seen before. At the very top of the atrium, mounted on the wall to my right as I gaze up, there's an immense digital clock, like those at stadiums, football fields, track meets. Its high tech display differs sharply from the frozen, outmoded clock on the old gym wall. The numbers it displays are moving, ticking off seconds, minutes, of achievement. Here is what I suddenly feel. I'm on a playing field. I'm down at the starting line. The floors of the store as they circle the atrium heading upwards are the track along which I'll race. The unavoidably upward movement becomes an embodied metaphor for achievement. The track is made literal by the shiny blond surface, as wide as a real track, which rings each floor just inside the guardrails. Solitary words shine up from the track surface: courage, victory. The insistence of the clock triggers my adrenalin as if I were waiting for the starting gun. The swoosh collapses into the space again, the infectious pound, the aural power, getting me ready to go, while the lyrics of the techno pop tell me to, "Seize the chance to see the limits stretched. Never stop. Get to the finish line. Anything less is to sacrifice your gifts." And so, when the screen rolls up, up I go. I'm not really running, but I feel as if I am: pound, breathe, pound, breathe, run, run, stretching the limits, that's the goal, the mark, the possibility, the becoming. The stakes are high, I feel the tension and the adrenalin, I really do.

This body, my body, as explicitly *matter*, as the site of sensation, is central to Massumi's formulation of affect, and through it the possibility of change. For him, affect illuminates the problem of how matter can move elsewhere from the place it has been affixed. Affect is the way that the body gives a kind of slip to its own position. This retrieval of the materiality of the body stands in contrast to most cultural theory, where the body is understood as an instance of discursive production, capable of moving only between cultural and ideological coordinates on a fixed grid. Without a way, or a willingness, to grasp the body as a material site of sensation, and without returning what is "most directly corporeal back into the body" (Massumi 2002: 4), "the very notion of movement as qualitative transformation is lacking" (Massumi 2002: 3).

Both Massumi and Taussig are politically progressive thinkers. For each, one with affect and the other with mimesis, transformation, as a process of the somatic affinities of a sensate, material body, is linked to the possibility of changing certain oppressive political, economic, or social practices. This progressive desire, however, has clearly not disqualified the processes which they so aptly identify from being used for quite different ends; the yielding of the body, the plasticity of identification and identity, the slip into aliveness, are a value-producing labor for the corporations – an ungridding which, in a point to which I've already alluded and to which I will return, is also the product we are making: grafting into ourselves, as ourselves, a pleasure in the indeterminacy and motion upon which contemporary global capital feeds.

Each floor of the store, each phase of the ascent, the track, underscores the feeling of stretching the limits, of moving else-where. The open atrium invites me to continuously check how far I've come and how far I have yet to go. The clock ticks. I never lose the sensation of the ascent I'm making, even when I linger. And the displays on the floors, each of which is organized around a different sport, carry the feeling of change and movement as their thematic. This is especially true of exhibits throughout the store, in which bones and musculature are graphically exposed in stages of being perfected by the precise application of advanced scientific principles. The biological human body morphs into a better version of itself through the intercession of the Nike brand. The body, in Nike, as Nike, can give itself the slip. In one display the human foot, its anatomy exposed, changes gradually, frame by frame, into a Nike shoe. Science and technology operate synonymously to trigger in me a narrative that accompanies my mimetic, affectual response. It triggers a deeply implicit under-standing that the network of technological practice, represented in a highly aesthetisized and pleasurable form here in this brand-scape, is the medium of my unfixing. A sign in the store reads:

> Athletes are dedicating themselves to training like never before. Armed with the knowledge of sports science, they are discov-ering new strength, speed and stamina. For the bar forever rises, and these are five athletes who continue to push it higher.

Large chrome capsules move up and down around me. Shoes are delivered by high tech capsules shot up from some invisible region. The word engineered is everywhere. My body is wrapped into a digital sizing machine. I feel the palpable sense of my own becoming better. I'm keeping on the move, going round and round, up and up. Although I'm above it now, I hear the swoosh come again, always that slamming heartbeat, and I feel myself in a posi-tion to truly aspire to the sentiment expressed in lyrics that I hear in fragments: "no more jealousy, hate, anger, loneliness, fear."

On the floor for all-terrain sports, I try on a pair of what might in the past have been hiking boots. This footwear is something I fail to recognize. I find that I want it anyway. I want it because when its futuristically engineered contours wrap my foot, I'll become a different, better kind of mountain climber. I can play as if I am what I am not. I am deeply attached to actual mountains that I often visit. But with my foot trying on this Nike foot, I don't feel the call of my mountains. Instead I feel the tangible call of mountains invented by Nike, an invention whose facticity I make real in this Nike skin. I've moved across a spectrum of the really made up. These are mountains given to me as that which I have the strength to succeed in surmounting, leaving old limitations in the past. I place my foot over the glass inset in the wooden floor. Just below the glass are beautiful stones, like those in the thin, wide stretches of water far above timberline. When I look down at my foot over these stones, in this boot, I see a foot that holds the power of what Nike can make it become: strong, vital, free from constriction, moving off the grid.

Finally, I reach the top, the fifth floor. And here the techno wrap evaporates. It's gone. The marvelous trajectory of my future-becoming, the bubble of the store, ends, surprisingly, by restoring me back to the space of the old gym. Here, again, is the faded brick of that space far below. The steel girders of the store are gone, the chrome, the glass. In place of all this is a simple wooden ceiling crisscrossed with pipes and air ducts. A pair of old fashioned, worn sneakers hangs by its joined laces from a duct pipe, cast-offs from an archaic world. I'm delivered afresh to the point of departure, that made up past. I measure how far it is from me; I'm different than I was at the starting line. I've lived the seductions of Nike movement. A sign encourages me to keep on moving. It reads: "There is no finish line." I can see that those stained canvas shoes are the mark of a past which has little to do with the passages and potentials I am enlivened by, in Nike, as Nike, playing Nike as if it were real.

Use-value: the alibi of an outside (where I am not locked in by the market)

This experience at Niketown, this tremendous *gut-feeling* response, may be further contextualized by suggesting that entertainment retail environments depend upon a particular relation between use and exchange value that is an underlying energy of the global scene in which we find ourselves. A look at use-value will also help us to frame an answer to the question of how through our productive capacity we create revenue shared in common across brands.

Use-value, in the simplest terms, refers to the intrinsic usefulness of a thing based in its material nature. For instance, when people make a table because they need a table to use in their kitchen, that table has a use-value.[3] Here a person's needs directly or "naturally" correspond to the intrinsic value of an object. Capitalism, though, is driven by exchange-value, in which the value of a commodity is based on units of an abstracted measure of the human labor that went into their making; socially necessary labor time. In this system, use-value is made instrumental on behalf of exchange-value. It also becomes abstract as it's separated from its original sense of an object made in response to actual need. According to Jean Baudrillard, use-value is an invention that creates the pretense that a particular product, circulating according to its exchange-value, is of use. It's an alibi the market depends on to grease the wheels of the purchase, materializing the exchange-value of the merchandise. It's only a system of apparent needs, answerable by products or brands. It's the made up reason why I should buy this product or fall for this brand.

For Baudrillard this network of needs is deeply connected to subjectivity, or the shapes and forms in which people appear and it is here that his theory becomes applicable to our productive capacity in Niketown and other brandscapes. He says we have a "faculty of pleasure" (Baudrillard 1981: 136) through which we work to bring ourselves forth as a person who affirms what we apparently needed; the use-value of the brand. The faculty of pleasure is a form of immaterial labor. We're "hired" to make good on the alibi, to be its proof. I don't really need to try on Nike, to feel the intense pleasure of my potential to move into a techno future of physical prowess. But at Niketown I labor, with my faculty of pleasure, to bring myself into being as a person who *does* need it. Being at Niketown is so pleasurable, I don't want to imagine, in that hour or so, being without the tremendous high that I am in the process of trying on, bringing into embodiment. I have a faculty of pleasure, for pleasure, for making pleasure; the brandscape architects induce it through my mimetic faculty and my sensation of affect. On my body, in my body, Nike feels essential.

The achievement of postmodern capitalism is to have so comprehensively generated and mobilized our productive capacity across so many social fields. Though there may be remnants of the ideology of the unified, stable self, capital does not really trade in them. We labor at multiple, shifting and provisional materializations of brand usefulness. We come into being through a bodily responsiveness to the brand, materializing its allure in the cellular structure of our bodies. We prove, thereby, that it is an answer to our needs. What would Nike do without me? I am an intrinsic part of the market's operations, bound into its systems of circulation, exchange and consumption.

Use-value had repeatedly been invoked, in various formulations, to suggest the possibility of an outside to the capitalist market. By claiming that there is such a thing as use-value that can be kept separate from exchange, people have thought that we might find a place to be free of capital, or bring forces to bear on it that can disrupt it. Hardt and Negri (2000: 208), for instance, note how the proletariat, traditionally, imagines itself as having a use-value, a position outside the exploitation of its labor that can make it autonomous from that exploitation.

But in the face of so much evidence that postmodern capitalism has comprehensively appropriated use-value as an alibi, it is hard to imagine that it can offer an alternative. Hardt and Negri (2000: 208–9), like Baudrillard (1981), strenuously argue that radical thought must be cleared of any attachment to the category of use-value as a potentially revolutionary position. *However*, following suggestions made by Susan Willis (1991: 13), I will argue here that what unifies the agendas of many different brands is that each of them triggers in us a kind of residual or remnant longing for a use-value that *is* an outside. After all, we are not insensate to the way in which we are bound and tied to the market. It might not be too much to suggest that we suffer, on a mass scale, from our sense of this; the United States is a nation afflicted with an epidemic of depression and anxiety, our knowledge that we are only as valuable as escaping the next downsizing or the next cuts in Medicaid.

Brandscapes offer us a chance to manufacture, in our mimetic and affectual labor, in the palpable medium of our flesh-full bodies, in our faculty of pleasure, a feeling of being free of the threats lurking in our constrained lives. When we make this feeling, it feels like escape, like a place outside the market. We're making an uber use-value for the brand – we're creating the feeling that we need the brand because it slips us off the grid. We're bringing forth moments that make us feel *as if* we are not fully integrated components of a market apparatus.

Corporations, taken as a whole, create grinding conditions of existence that drain life of its vivacity. But at the same time each offers a brand whose use-value is materialized in our mimetic bodies as proof that the brand is actually the source of liveliness, change, and possibility, an escape to an outside. When Hoke refers to how the brandscape needs to sow the seeds of the brand deep into the consumer for future harvest, this is the harvest he means. Our own productive capacities are the source for making the brand the (only) hope for escape from the deadening effects of being trapped, maybe below the poverty line, in stressful or tedious jobs, where we're at the mercy of market forces, hooked in twenty-four/ seven via blackberries, laptops, and cell phones, experiencing the shrinking of life's liveliness to shopping, the Internet, the iPod network, the video game. This is the reason, we could speculate, that most people in the United States (as one of the places in the world where the consumption strategies of capital are most effectively practiced) come back to branded experiences again and again. Movement is the collective alibi of the brands, the convincing face by which they exact their seductions. People want to feel alive. The brand makes a place for them to feel as if they were. And where else would they go?

To sum up thus far, let us say that in brandscapes we produce use-value through our somatic absorption or trying on of the brand. We can term the means of production our faculty of pleasure, a bodily labor which produces immaterial things; feelings, affinities, memories, desires. The use-value that we make might be defined generally as a vivacity that creates a sense of potential and movement, a somatic wonder that makes us feel free of the constrictions of the market. In the store, we live that use-value, in all our mimetic creativity, as if it were real.

However, even if we say that this sense of our potential movement is a kind of uber use-value that is made in all brandscapes, we can also say that each store has its own speciality in this regard. For instance, the use-value of Niketown is feeling oneself move along a passage toward a futural, techno self. The passage, the affectual movement at the Ralph Lauren flagship store, is of a different kind. In this store people play as if it they were able to move among categories of class identification. Either way, the brand is the fleshed out fullness of being's potential to be other, life's vivacity.

Historical echoes

The Alchemist

Ben Jonson's play, *The Alchemist* (1610), can be read as a study of the way even early modern subjectivity begins to be organized thru the faculty of pleasure. In the play, a trio of down-and-out hucksters, Dol (a prostitute), and Subtle and Face (who pimp for her), set themselves up for business in the London house vacated for a time by Face's master, who is in flight from the plague. In this urban comedy set in Jonson's London, each of the trio is a theatrical being who, with this scheme, is able to change faces effectively in order to take advantage of the new circulation of currency, people, and investment. The scheme is spearheaded by Subtle, who is posing as a pious, humble and pure alchemist with a headful of erudite knowledge and formulas. His only actual alchemical translation is turning the gullibility of his customers into capital accumulation.

As an alchemist, Subtle's products can be credibly immaterial. That is, his customers can be convinced to buy something that they may never actually see, or whose properties may be invisible to them. In this way, his products draw uncannily close to the postmodern brand. Subtle markets his products by inducing in his customers a vision of the self they will be able to become under the influence of the product. Not only is there no actual use-value in his products, but also there is no product at all. There are only customers who labor to bring themselves into being in shapes that will confirm that the product is vital to them, necessary to their well-being. The allure of the [imaginary] product will be materialized in the form of their new selves.

Subtle is selling Mammon, a knight, and Tribulation, a Puritan, a "philosopher's stone." Mammon is already puffing himself up – enhanced a hundredfold, sexually and in wealth. He will be proof of the stone's usefulness (and credibility) in that he will have "a list of wives and concubines / Equal with Solomon, who had the stone /Alike with me; and I will make me a back / With the elixer, that shall be as tough /As Hercules, to encounter fifty a night" (Jonson 1979: 198). He'll gallantly defend the honor of ladies done in by "court stallions" by making of those fellows eunuchs who will "fan me with ten ostrich tails /A-piece, made in a plum to gather wind" (Jonson 1979: 199), proving that, "We will be brave, Puff, now we have the medicine" (Jonson 1979: 199). These fantasy embodiments of his courage are immediately followed by visions of himself at table, where he is master of the world's wealth: "My meat shall all come in, in Indian shells, / Dishes of agate set in gold, and studded /With emeralds, sapphires, hyacinths, and rubies" (Jonson 1979: 199).

Tribulation, the Puritan, will be proof of the stone's ability to procure for him and other Puritans a secure position of power; through Subtle's sales pitch, he sees himself already moving through the world winning friends by curing maladies and being able to pay whole armies by turning cheap metals into pure gold.

> *Subtle*:   Have I discoursed so unto you of our stone,
>   And of the good that it shall bring your cause? . . .
>   That even the medicinal use shall make you a
>   faction
>   And party in the realm? As, put the case,
>   That some great man in state, he have the gout,
>   Why, you but send three drops of your elixer,
>   You help him straight: there you have made a
>   friend.
>   Another has the palsy or the dropsy,
>   He takes of your incombustible stuff,
>   He's young again: there you have made a friend.
>   . . .
>   A lord that is a leper,
>   A knight that has the bone-ache, or a squire
>   That hath both these, you make them smooth and
>   sound,
>   With a bare fricace of your medicine: still
>   You increase your friends.
> *Tribulation*:   Aye, it is very pregnant.

> *Subtle*:   And then the turning of this lawyer's pewter
> To plate at Christmas
> . . .
> Or changing
> His parcel gift to massy gold. You cannot
> But raise you friends. Withal, to be of power
> To pay an army in the field, to buy
> The king of France out of his realms, or Spain
> Out of his Indies. What can you not do
> Against lords spiritual or temporal,
> That shall oppose you?
> *Tribulation*:   Verily, 'tis true.
> We may be temporal lords ourselves, I take it.
> *Subtle*:   You may be anything.
>   (Jonson 1979: 219–20)

For Draper, the gambler, Subtle is supposedly making a "familiar," or spirit guide. When Draper starts winning at the gaming tables, he will be living proof of the familiar's talents. Likewise, Drugger as a successful business man will be proof of the efficacy of the magical runes Subtle is allegedly fashioning to attract customers to Drugger's apothecary.

Subtle's customers all desire a transformation, a new state of being, a movement from where they are now to where they could be. In the case of each of these customers, Subtle interpolates as his sales strategy their pleasure in manufacturing themselves in the image that materializes the use-value, or alibi, of his product. With the help of his initial suggestions, they produce the alibi of his commodity for him, guaranteeing its exchange value: they pay him for it without it ever being a material, actual thing. Its use cannot be verified outside the bizarre new exchange economy into which these early modern characters are being inexorably drawn as the theatre helps to summon into being the practices of a commodity culture.

Ralph Lauren

Unlike Niketown on 57th Street, this flagship store is situated in a genuinely historic New York City edifice, one of the remaining grand mansions of Manhattan: 867 Madison Avenue was commissioned in 1895 by Gertrude Rhinelander-Waldo, a descendant of Philip Jacob Rhinelander, one of the largest landowners in the city. The mansion, designed in sixteenth-century French Renaissance/Gothic chateau style, was one of the biggest private homes in Manhattan. Rhinelander-Waldo, however, never did move in to the mansion. As it was being built, she toured Europe and purchased artwork and accessories for the home, but upon her return decided to live elsewhere. The house, increasingly dilapidated, and full of treasures that were gradually looted, remained empty until 1921, ten years after Rhinelander-Waldo died with a $150,000 outstanding mortgage.[4]

After 1921, the first floor of the mansion was used for retail, with the upper floors subdivided into apartments. When Ralph Lauren purchased the building, he began full-scale renovations that resulted in the opening of his store in 1986, which, despite Nike's claims to have invented the form, was the very first of themed retail built around one brand.

Lauren himself, as is fairly commonly known, was originally Ralph Lifschitz, a Jewish boy born to Russian immigrant parents in the Bronx. He is a model of self-fashioning, the undoing of fixed social identity into the performance of self. His occupation of the mansion, a signifier of great wealth lost to a bank foreclosure, suggests that the playing field can be leveled, that wealth is mutable. As he himself moved across social fields, so he had the mansion designed as space that offers anyone who enters its doors the chance to play *as if* he or she could do likewise (even as most people actually never will have a chance to do so).

It's a hot summer day when I first arrive at the mansion. The sidewalks outside are steamy and smelly, the New York humidity pressing down on all the shared public life being endured there. But once through the door, a strange physical relief saturates me, a sensation of sudden, total enfoldment in what I see, feel, smell and hear to be a luxurious space, cooled, hushed, and darkened. The foyer in which I stand, my eyes adjusting, is scented by the glorious bouquet of fresh flowers placed in an urn on a table at its center. There doesn't seem to be anything displayed for sale. If there is, it is not what I see.

What I do see, and begin gradually and increasingly to touch, is a richly and densely packed *household*. The personal effects of the people who seem to live here are everywhere. Every detail is intricate, thorough, and no detail is without the trace of its long use by someone in this home, a use that is, of course, made up. Ahead of me, at the base of the gorgeous curved stair, is a coat rack upon which are hanging a few worn coats, presumably those of someone who lives here. To my right, in a room off the foyer, in what appears to be a kind of sitting room for the gentleman of the house, there is a fire set ready to be lit and the mantle that frames it has numerous niches filled with personal effects, books and knickknacks. Over the mantle hangs a grand hunting picture in an eighteenth-century style, framed in gold gilt. The mantle itself is set with clock, candles, a small statue, a lovely box. The room has a glistening parquet floor. There are reading lamps lit over easy chairs, an invitation for a late afternoon with a book. A pair of slippers next to a chair seems to await the tired feet of its owner.

The House Palatial

The store that Lauren designed had its precedent in 1908, at Wanamakers. In the early twentieth century the leading theatre designers, Joseph Urban (principal designer for Zieg-feld), Lee Simonson and Norman Bel Geddes all designed enthusiastically for consumer interiors; themed environments extravagantly akin to contemporary brandscapes. Urban, for instance, declared that his intention for both retail and theatre design was to create spaces that people "could vicariously inhabit" (Leach 1993: 144). He rejected nineteenth-century theatrical realism and its painted sets, working instead with "light and color, the dramatization of spaces and objects and the forging of atmospheres" (Leach 1993: 145). Other theatre designers whose work was translated to consumer environments were those who, like Belasco and MacKaye, experimented with spectacular pictures, assemblages of tableaux, light, and scenery. This investment in atmospheric, three-dimensional environments that consumers could "inhabit" is particularly clear in the Wanamakers display. "The House Palatial," as it was called, was set down right at the center of the department store. It was a " 'real,' two-story, twenty-four room dwelling" that:

could have been lifted right off a Belasco or Mackaye stage. It held – among other features – staircases, a butler's pantry, a servant's dining quarters, an Elizabethan library decorated with tiger skins, a Jacobean dining room, a Louis XIV salon, and even a large Italian garden off the dining room. The set was decoratively lighted and looked lived in, with books tossed about and golf clubs propped against the walls. Complete assemblings of furniture, drapery, and art taken from departments throughout the store were set up in every room.

(Leach 1993: 80–1)

To grasp the way in which movement across class boundaries is the use-value that is produced in this store, it is helpful to refer to Pierre Bourdieu (1984). His concept of habitus helps to see the way that class is established in this brandscape, if only so that it can be traversed. Habitus refers to the combination of dispositions that distinguish members of one class, or class fraction, from another. These dispositions are tendencies among members of classes or class fractions to prefer some objects more than others, some forms of aesthetic consumption over others, some sports or foods over others. Habitus not only gathers dispositions into a common set of tendencies and characteristics, but also organizes them into a coherency that lends them the appearance of being inherent or natural qualities of the members of a particular class, masking the processes of class relations by which they are actually produced. The habitus is an active, generative space within which members of a certain class go about reproducing the signs of their distinction, their distinguishing dispositions. The Ralph Lauren store literalizes habitus as a physical space, reiterating the dispositions of the people who seem to live there through the objects and spatial relations that constitute it.

The habitus recreated by the store depends on a merger of two kinds of distinction. The first is the "aesthetic disposition," which refers to the high degree of education and cultural sophistication of those who possess it. As I will find in various rooms upstairs, the walls are hung with Mapplethorpe photographs, or a close-up of Michelangelo's *David*, a big soft armchair is snug up against a table stacked with a book on the Sex Pistols, on Picasso, a volume of John Dryden's poetry, CDs of Charlie Parker. A precondition of the aesthetic disposition is a distance from the world of economic necessity: a person distinguished by the aesthetic disposition responds to works of art almost exclusively as assemblages of form or style, disassociated from any social or political urgency.

The second disposition is based on a particular mode of acquisition, inheritance. This is acquisition of wealth by birth, the most legitimate means by which wealth belongs to one and which therefore confers more distinction than wealth gained through education, work, or luck. It means that the person to whom this wealth belongs has, through the line of inheritance, been entitled to wealth over a much longer period than the person who acquires it by other means. Control of wealth over time is constitutive of the most rarified of class dispositions (see Bourdieu 1984: 70). The aesthetic disposition is best cultivated as an aspect of inherited wealth, where a person is surrounded by the signs of capital inherited over time, and luxuriates in settings which invite the contemplation of art or the absorption of books, without any sense of having to do so for any particular purpose other than the nourishment of one's own self. Merged together, these dispositions form the habitus of the most elite populations in American society.

Along with the Mapplethorpe, the Charlie Parker, and the Georgia O'Keefe, the mansion is simultaneously saturated with age. The saturation begins, of course, with staging the habitus in a genuinely old building, a historic landmark. Throughout the interior, age is everywhere evident in the way that only the homes of the rich, those rich from "old" money, sometimes are. That is, exquisite, expensive objects, rather than being thrown out and replaced as they deteriorate, remain central in the décor of the household. Leather armchairs are cracked and peeling, and the silvering of the many mirrors is so deteriorated they reflect nothing. Umbrellas, battered and old, but expensive, made with carved wooden handles, stand in beautiful old brass stands. Under my feet the kilim rugs, the real thing, are threadbare.

It is also true that the antique valises, the encrusted shells, the zebra skins, and the maps that casually dress shelves or mantles throughout the store are references to the pleasures of the wealthy. They've been able to travel, explore, and collect across various historical periods in ways that ordinary people have not. It is also a reference to the history of colonialism and imperialism in which the inherited wealth that distinguishes the wealthy originates.

But the age of the objects simultaneously distances that history from the occupants of the house. The evocation of world domination in the past is necessary because the history of that domination is a marker of the control of wealth over time. Here in the home, though, it has taken on the benign qualities of aesthetic décor. Domination is translated into the language of nature love, rustic simplicity and the evocative aesthetic power of the antique.

One of the most remarkable rooms of the house assembles the signs of these dispositions with an incredible lushness, and it can begin to illustrate how the habitus opens itself so that I can traverse it, play as if I could become a member of it. For the strangest thing about this room, high on the third floor, and about the house in general, is how it has been evacuated of its inhabitants. The table in this shuttered room seems set for me. Whose feet are those emptied slippers, waiting downstairs by the reading chair, waiting for? Is it I for whom this is intended? Is it I who has arrived home? This does indeed seem to be the way that the store is designed. Throughout the store it is as if the occupants of the home have suddenly evaporated, leaving me in their place. What were their shoes are now mine to move in to, their food mine to eat, their beds mine to sleep in, their books mine to read, their scents the balm for my frayed nerves. I find that, even though there are other performers/consumers in the space, the dense somatic allure of each object, each setting, sucks me into a kind of vortex of response from which others disappear.

The third floor room is actually more like an installation meant to transport me out of this mansion and into an entirely different world. (The suggestion and trajectory of movement is continually present.) This room has a double evocation: evacuated of inhabitants, except for me, it is as if I had been able to go to where the members of this family go, when they travel, collect, explore. It is also a kind of time-warped, oxymoronic version of where they might have luxuriated as colonial masters, brought close to but remaining absolutely separate from the exploitation that enriches them. The two times, the two kinds of collecting are brought close into the unfolding of this really made up habitus, with me as its protagonist, its actor, its person-in-becoming.

The room is actually a suite of two rooms – a dining room and a bedroom – joined by a short hallway. The rooms are a combination of all my personal favorites, a chance to feel myself moving into who I might wish to be, feeling it in my body, bringing it

close: Mediterranean, French Provincial, and the American South-
west. The scene is spectacularly layered with roughly hewn wooden
beams, tile floors, adobe walls, cast iron chandeliers, dried bunches
of lavender and flax, worn and frayed straw mats on the floor, a
four-poster canopy bed hung in Indian cloth upon which rests a
tray with half-eaten red pears (is it I who ate them, or who will
eat the next bite?), and a flask of wine, one vaguely Arab slipper
casually thrown beside it (mine?), live potted palms, live potted
herbs, dark wooden shutters closed (against the harsh sun), huge
fireplace surrounded by a rough pine mantle, stacks of firewood
decorated with dried flowers of all kinds, peeling plaster, hemp
rope, beautiful old baskets, pottery and ceramics, antique French
Provincial furniture, a dried hornet's nest, encrusted shells, Tom
Waits over the speakers, mysterious, ripped and faded old black
and white photographs, huge old books on esoteric subjects in
faded and torn yellowish covers, and, on the table and sideboard,
an extravagance of food – more red pears, cheeses, artichokes,
dates, French wine (in bottle and huge flasks marked generically
"Vin du Provence"), and fresh breads, all of which are real, fresh,
overflowing with invitation. The live-ness of it, the bodily-ness
of it, are irresistible. It is impossible for me not to pull close into
it, and feel, as a result, that I am moving away from who I am
or was. I am someone who can understand all this, appreciates it,
who dwells within it as naturally as if it were air.

The colonial/imperial history to which the room is attached is
unspecified. The shuttered, floor to ceiling windows, the potted
palm, the frayed hemp rugs evoke the Caribbean, Central America,
or Africa. The place simultaneously produces the signs of where
the wealth has come from and what can be gotten with the wealth.
The sugar cane fields running on near slave labor, for instance,
might be just on the other side of those shutters as I luxuriate with
all that the wealth extracted from the labor in those fields bring
to me; the artichokes, the wine, the fine cheeses, the panoply of
world fabrics and textures and tastes. To get to the top of the
capitalist hierarchy is to emerge outside its hardships, humiliations
and entrapments. I live off those still trapped inside it, still on the
grid. I feel that the room defines how far I can and do move from
the sweating workers outside those shuttered windows, how distant
from the violent sharpness of cane that cuts the flesh.

Bourdieu claims that habitus is a "site of durable solidarities"
(Bourdieu 2000: 145); that the body is attached on a gut level to

the set of social relations which constitute it and that this gut level connection is a loyalty that can't be undone. But what if, by contrast, this store provides the means for each performer/ consumer to feel in his or her self a membership in this dominant class habitus, to feel it in such a rich way that it feels deeply inscribed? What if it offers bodily, sensate, mimetic, and affectual play in the really made up so as to produce in me the sensation of habitus uprooted from its moorings? What if the point is to offer habitus as something that can be played rather than something which is a deep-rooted apparatus of social identity? By recreating the most rarified habitus, the one that seems most unattainable, the store suggests this possibility even more adamantly. I can try on, in the physiology of my own body, even those dispositions that take generations and generations to get right. The store creates the visceral bodily conditions through which habitus is made up but it simultaneously produces the feeling of undoing habitus so that we can play as if social hierarchies were not so fixed. We labor, through our faculty of pleasure, to bring forth in our bodies a movement-slip across habitus. I am not I, here. I am in a space of emergence because all has been readied for me to play as if I were someone else, as if I were the kind of person who could live in a place like this.

Here is an important point about the really made up. Its pleasure lies in its staying as just that. I don't actually reach out and eat the foods, or really lie down on the beds. At the margin of doing so lies the real, whereas the really made up is the space of production for the faculty of pleasure. The presence of the real food, its viscerally tangible closeness, the lushness of its beauty is all I need to play the really made up, to get it in my body. I know that in the real I can't move much. If I were to take an artichoke leaf, break the bread, it is likely that some store attendant would materialize from an inconspicuous haunt and ask me to leave the store. The real would come crashing in. Not eating preserves me in the space of the really made up where I can feel *as if* I can move, a different place from my ordinary life. For this reason, I am learning to prefer the really made up. This is the unspoken contract between me and the corporation.

So here is how I play the really made up. Here is how I can move, what I can play as if I could become. I can drift through the first floor of the space, stroking the smooth wood of a table, bending to smell flowers, resting for a moment in a beautiful old chair while my eyes drift over paintings, and, after a while, I float movie star style up the lustrous staircase to the second floor, feeling as if the train of my exquisite evening dress were draped over the steps behind my languid and elegant body, watched over by the progenitors whose portraits in oils adorn the walls. After the second floor, I will ascend to the third and then the fourth by the inner staircases, darkened and softened with plush, sound absorbing carpeting, the scent of age and memory, and hung with the painted scenes of violence and dominion, made benign by their stillness, which comfort and name the people associated with this home: paintings of men on horses, riding crops in hand, hunting dogs with bloody birds in their jaws, more progenitors, fishing scenes, fish hung by hooks, western landscapes, captured. I move through the most interior domesticity, and feel the dark, quiet heart of the home.

The second, third and fourth floors of the mansions are elegant interiors, with carved white ceilings, crystal chandeliers, and small rooms opening off a grand center hallway. The second floor is for men, the third for women and children, and the fourth for linens. I go all the way to the top, to the bedroom, to a four-poster bed lavishly dressed in pink linens. Next to the bed is a night table with a tray with champagne, champagne glasses and pistachio nuts. Ballerinas in pink and gray sepia tones dance across the wall, frozen in artful photographs. Other tables are strewn with art and photography books: Cartier-Bresson, Picasso. I love these books. I could sink into one of these pink chairs and stay forever. I hate pink. Here I find it tasteful. Across from the bedroom there is a small sitting room with a round table for two in white linens, two chairs, pink peonies and a plate of pink meringues. I love meringues. I can feel their taste on my tongue. Behind the table, there's a glorious spray of white dogwood blossoms, one of my favorite of all the spectacles of spring.

All this is far from my own habitus. My life, for instance, has none of the inherited acquisition, the control of wealth over time, which saturates this space. My grandparents were the working poor, uneducated past fourth grade, did not know Cartier-Bresson, never tried meringues, decorated their house with plastic flowers, ate pies made from apples from the tree in their backyard, slept under quilts handmade from bits of old clothes, everything re-cycled, made to serve again, nothing thrown away. But I breathe deep, inhaling the smell of lilies, the fresh, cooled air. I take on in my mimetic body the sensation of traversal. The feel of the heavy wool of a homemade grandmother's quilt, embedded in me, shifts, and maybe evaporates, as I stroke the smooth surfaces of Ralph Lauren; the pink bed, the velvet chair. This really made up moment is saturated with affect; a charged vitality. Luxury, freedom from care, an enclave from the sordidness of the world, retreat and refreshment, spring any time I order it from the florist; these can be my birthright here.

In conclusion: Empire and the seductions of being on the move

The intense pleasure of mimetic play with our own unstructured potential, especially as it causes us to sense a move outside our daily constrictions, creates the alibi for the brand. It's what makes us value the brand and return to it again and again. The mimetic nature of our immaterial labor is such that we take intense pleasure in the really made up, that bodily experienced spectrum between facticity and invention, which is the space of movement and change. Ralph Lauren made himself up, we know the home in the mansion is made up, and we know that our mimetic and affectual experience within it is made up, but, the fact that we can and do feel ourselves moving in our sensate, somatic being along this spectrum between facticity and invention both promises and materializes the real-ness of our potential to change.

Given the corporate context within which our mimetic work takes place, however, we can assume that with each play at moving outside constriction we are being further embedded into a logic of containment. I've argued that the seduction of being on the move is an uber use-value that produces revenue across corporations because it makes us understand the brand in general as the place, the only place, where we can come free of the grid. But there are other benefits that global capital in general reaps from our productive capacity in brandscapes. The movement slip that we bring forth there through our faculty of pleasure corresponds to changes in the organization and nature of economic production and changes in the production of subjectivity wrought in the transition to Empire.

First, there is a transition away from industrial economic production at geographically locatable and longstanding sites and toward a decentralized system of production in which workers in widely dispersed places are linked in a horizontal network of communication. This means that we must learn to understand ourselves and what we do as dislodged from any of the traditional moorings upon which the old proletariat could depend. Often moving frequently between low paying service jobs, or even high paying corporate jobs as corporations merge and move, we increasingly experience ourselves as circulating nodal points between which information and capital pass. In what we do each day, geography, and the rooted identity it could form, has less and less meaning.[5] The world takes on the appearance of the invisible and almost instantaneous flow and movement through which capital travels, as the biopolitical power of Empire transforms the world into its own image. This is as true for "white collar" workers sitting at computers on trains, in homes, on airplanes, sending their ideas and information zinging across the world as it is for those who labor in the industrial sector. Factories disappear from one place one day and reappear across the globe the next with the workers who are left behind understanding that to remain viable they have to keep on the move in capital's forced migratory flows.[6]

Second, in the transition from disciplinary society to the "society of control" (Hardt and Negri 2000: 329–32), the production of subjectivity changes. Once formed by the discourses of discreet institutions whose logics were often separate – the school, the church, the family – subjectivity is now an effect of those institutions losing their boundaries, both discursive and geographical, and becoming themselves hyperlinked, networked, and overlaid. The imperial subject, as opposed to the disciplinary one, is "hybrid and modulating . . . produced simultaneously by numerous institutions in different combinations and doses" (Hardt and Negri 2000: 331). As I've said, from its inception capital sought to construct subjectivity as a flexible, fluid and playable thing. Imperial capital marks an intensification of this historical relationship, even over that of the postmodernity of the last decades of the twentieth century. Through our faculty of pleasure we bring ourselves into being as the principle of fluidity itself, restless motion, underdeveloped, always moving elsewhere, ready to be redeployed, reenlisted as a new face, a new source of production. We are incorporated vascularly into capital as we circulate through its passageways, responsible for every aspect of what it needs to thrive.

Branded environments, more specifically, are both a rehearsal for and an actualization of the dissolution of the institutional sites for the production of disciplined subjectivity. They are the model for the hybrid, multiple, creative, constantly changing social terrains across which we are encouraged to travel. In one day, a single performer/consumer might travel from Niketown, to Ralph Lauren, to American Girl Place, and in each one play as if she were a completely different being. In this way subjectivity is itself proposed and rehearsed as the principle of flexible hybridity, while at the same time, at each site, this performer/consumer is bringing into being through her embodiment the working premises of the particular corporation: a valorization of a techno-futural hyper-athletic being, the mutability of social hierarchy, or the challenging forth of the human being as American, as we shall see in Chapter 4. These premises themselves are highly flexible and can disappear in a day, or be quickly supplanted by others. (This is why these environments tend to be so fleeting.) The productive social terrain of the society of control, unlike the institutions of the society of discipline, is highly responsive to change, capital flow, changing networks of information or production. Likewise, subjectivity needs to be maintained in an indeterminate state so that humans too can be shifted, moved, and repositioned quickly and easily according to the shifting flows of capital.

This is why the production of affect is becoming so dominant as a mode of immaterial production in Empire. Affect is the production of the enlivening charge of indeterminacy. We gravitate to this charge. We agree, in the stores, to become the very laborers who produce it in ourselves and then to say to ourselves that this is why we needed the brand all along. It is an alibi indispensable to power. Massumi remarks that: "The ability of affect to produce an economic effect more swiftly and surely than economics itself means that affect is a real condition, an intrinsic variable of the late capitalist system, as infrastructural as a factory" (Massumi 2002: 45).

It is of course true that companies are still dependent on selling commodities. Nike still needs us to buy shoes. But that's not the purpose of the brandscapes, and it's maybe not even what is most important to the development of capital at this juncture. What corporations are focused on is their harvest of our own production of brands, collectively, as the source of life, of liveliness, and of our attendant production of ourselves in shapes that mirror the fluid indeterminacy of global capital. I walk away from the store, we all walk away from the store, into the varied circumstances of lives situated in the economic, spiritual, political and cultural impoverishment that corporate hegemony is steadily surrounding us with. We may buy a child, or ourselves, a pair of Nike shoes at Foot Locker – maybe because that's what Foot Locker sells, maybe because the shoes are cool, maybe because there's brand recognition, or even because we attach an echo of the affectual charge Nike gives us to the shoes. This purchase may still be the bread and butter of Nike. But the big brands are investing a great deal in making me productive in a very different way. I, we, want to, and do, go back to the stores, over and over. It's there we get our best shot at our potential for change and movement. The swoosh pumps my blood and so I'm ready to go, I'm moving on, I'm feeling life's vivacious charge. And so, I'm a fully corporate player. I'm off the grid. In breaking free I'm failing to notice how my capacity to imagine real political and economic change atrophies with every swoosh, every red pear, and waiting slipper.

Chapter 2

Robots, gods and greed

The theatrum mundi in the Forum Shops at Caesar's Palace

Setting the stage

It's 104 degrees in Las Vegas, white hot heat. I've come here to study the Forum Shops, the shopping mall that opens into Caesar's Palace casino.

I'm carried into the mall on a long, moving walkway suspended over impossibly blue water. The blue is complemented by the pristine white of the knock-off Roman architecture that supports the walkway and the perfect green of palm trees and topiaries. It's a passageway out of the geography of Nevada, that collection of wrecked and parched upheavals of wrinkled rock.

Inside, I find myself in what appears to be a recreation of the Trajan's Market in Rome, circa AD 110. That ancient market was built adjacent to Emperor Trajan's forum. It was a curved, domed, two-story structure with shops lining both levels. Nowadays, much of it lies in ruins, but its structure is still observable. At Caesar's Palace, the ruins have been reassembled, the friezes restored. There is the same two-story structure, the arched openings, the dome, and the columns. The place is crowded with Romanesque statuary, grouped in the central plazas and in the niches in the walls. Standing gracefully on top of the stores, silhouetted against the blue sky, are statues that seem to be the assembled Roman gods. They are spaced regularly, their feet just touching the roofs of the shops. They look down on us, watching.

Many of the stores are high-end boutiques, most of the rest are outposts of the branded superstore. Nike is there, along with Disney and Warner Brothers. All the entrances to these stores, as well as the stores' interiors, are themed to match the Roman motif. For instance, the protruding marquee marking the entrance to the

Disney store serves as the stage for this odd pastiche: an Olympian-esque torch of gigantic proportions, a Pegasus with wings ready for flight, seeming to draw behind it in a little chariot Minnie and Mickey, who wave out to the mall, like touring royalty. A "frieze" inside the store features a comic character saturnalia. Mickey, Goofy, Donald and company, festooned in olive leaves, are reveling at a feast of hot dogs, pizza, bologna sandwiches, and a still living lobster. Inside, a huge Roman soldier's helmet hangs suspended over the central arc of cash registers. On either side of its golden fiberglass plume, it has Mickey ears. And down one avenue of this marketplace, the mall opens into Caesar's Palace Casino, a huge cavity, itself, of course, dressed in Romanesque motifs.

At each end of the mall there is a large, circular fountain called "The Fountain of the Gods." High on a central pedestal, sur-rounded by arcs of water shooting toward the base of the pedestal, sits a bland, white, fiberglass statue of Bacchus, complete with a wine goblet. Behind him, poised at the edge of the fountain, is a statue of Venus. Opposite Venus, across the fountain, is a statue of Apollo, holding a lute. But this isn't just a fountain. It's also a stage. Every half hour, these statues come to life to perform the "Festival Fountain Show." As a rousing orchestral score begins, Bacchus is the first to move into action. He is the master of cere-monies, and the pedestal on which he sits begins to move in a circle so that he can greet all of us, who are surrounding the foun-tain. This little god is predictably olive-leaf festooned, with a rotund belly naked and overflowing his draped garments. He lifts his goblet to us, bends and tilts stiffly, turning his blind head from one side to another, leering with his robotic mouth. He begins to speak, a great deep voice over the music: "Great pleasures await, step forward, one and all, into the mall," where waiting for us are "wonders of pageantry." With a gesture from Bacchus, Apollo now jerks roughly into motion, his stiff fingers strumming mech-anically over his lute. "Apollo," Bacchus gushes, "come join my guests. Favor our friends with a magical melody, music to enchant and inspire." Then he calls to Venus, "goddess of love, whose beauty dazzles and delights." She begins to bend and lilt toward us. With all three now in motion, Bacchus sends his voice soaring over the music. Laughing in delight, he cries out, "Let the festivities begin!"

This little god and the way he scripts our passage through the mall is at the core of my analysis of this environment. First, though,

I'll place him in the larger context of this casino driven city. So much is said about Las Vegas – its tacky fun and its fantasy-driven pleasures. I want to push in a different direction, seeing this mall as yet another unfolding of the brandscape phenomenon I am studying more generally. To do so, I address the tensions raised by the theatrical relation between the real and the fake in Las Vegas, and how fantasy here is not so harmless but unravels into the social consequences of the embodied imagination.

The new Las Vegas: the undoing of the real

Las Vegas is a city famous, or notorious, for its instantiation of the postmodern play with the "real" original, for its quotations of history and geography, and for the intense pleasure people take in visiting a place where, as in the theatre, everything is made up.

Since the 1970s, designers of Las Vegas environments, like those of brandscapes, have drawn on explicitly theatrical models. Venturi, Brown, and Izenour, in their classic book on architecture from 1972, *Learning from Las Vegas*, hinted at the upcoming transition to theatrical absorptions that these designers would implement. They describe the city they encountered at the beginning of the 1970s as consisting of casinos that were low, flat, brown buildings distinguished from the surrounding Mojave desert by the size and placement of their neon signs. Las Vegas was at the time a car culture and the competing signs were meant to lure people driving by in their cars into one casino over another. As such, the signs mattered much more than the architecture of the casinos.

But this was soon to change. The introduction of port cocheres to the hotels marked the beginning of the engulfment of the visitor in a role as the dominant tendency of a new Las Vegas. Rather than parking the car and walking across the parking lot to the casino, the port cochere allowed the visitor to drive right into the ostentatious environment of the hotel's entrance. Caesar's Palace, for instance, sported a series of fountains that lined an entry drive along which limousines pulled up to costumed doormen.

The drive-up entryways, which reconfigured the visitor's arrival as their entrance, the start of their performance, initiated a new kind of competition among the new casinos/hotels. Each vied for who could create the most thoroughly elaborated narration through which visitors could begin to reimagine their economic and social classification, the translation of everyman into king. Venturi, Brown and Izenour, observing at the onset of this change, wrote that Las Vegas was becoming a place where:

> [E]ssential to the imagery of the pleasure zone is the ability to engulf the visitor in a new role – for three days he may imagine himself a centurion at Caesar's Palace, a ranger at the frontier, or a jet-setting playboy at the Riviera.
>
> (Venturi *et al.* 1972: 58)

Writing about Sarno, the architect of Caesar's Palace, Alan Hess says:

> [H]e emphasized that anyone in the mass market could be a Caesar with this as his palace. Sarno's dream enveloped visitors in a total environment intended to transport them from reality to fantasy. Psychologically, the fantastic resorts distanced customers from the everyday world and the concerns which might put a break on their gambling.
>
> (Hess 1993: 85)

Like themed entertainment retail, or brandscapes, the casinos were becoming places of performance, mimetically charged environments for the trying on of other identities.

Following Sarno's lead, the old casinos were demolished, the signs sent to the Las Vegas sign graveyard, and Las Vegas materialized in the general outline of its current form. It is now an assemblage of themed buildings, a geographical and historical hit parade, ransacked from across the globe. There is, for instance, the Luxor casino, built as a pyramid with an Egyptian theme throughout. More recently, the Bellagio and the Venetian have made their appearance on The Strip, with the Bellagio offering the pleasures of a Tuscan villa, and the Venetian the sights of a replicated Venice, complete with indoor canals and gondolas.

Significantly, the themed environments are designed to be experienced by pedestrians rather than by motorists. The car has disappeared as a central element of Las Vegas so that the symbolic and actual space once devoted to it is reworked as a space for the imaginative possibilities of embodied performances of the really made up.[1] Space and structures are designed so that in their scripted movement through them, visitors experience them as stages and become performing consumers.

The ebullient, anarchic growth of pastiche in Las Vegas has many critics, especially among those who, like architecture critic Ada Louise Huxtable, are offended by the disappearance of what they consider to be the real. Huxtable (1997) laments the loss of aura – understood, since Walter Benjamin's use of the term, as the singularity of an original object. She resents the fake, the product of the non-auratic, reproduction-based ethos of capitalist culture. Oddly enough, in the following statement she seems initially drawn to the fake. She seems to be interested in the way that it can slide into the real, creating the oxymoronic category of what she calls the "real fake":

> The real fake reaches its apogee in places like Las Vegas, where it has been developed into an art form. The purpose is clear and the solution is dazzling; the result is completely and sublimely itself. The outrageously fake has developed its own indigenous style and lifestyle to become a real place.
>
> (Huxtable 1997: 1)

But, as she goes on, she makes explicit use of the theatre as her grounds for criticizing the fake in Las Vegas. It become clear that for her the fake, like the theatre, or "playacting," erases the deeper truths of the real through its inadequate copying. She describes Freemont Street, the old downtown of Las Vegas, as "linear urban theatre" (Huxtable 1997: 1), where the fake is the imagination gone bad, producing offensive copies of a more permanent reality. She says:

> Architecture and the environment as packaging or playacting, as disengagement from reality, is a notion whose time, alas, seems to have come. Environment is entertainment and artifice. Give or take demolition and natural disasters, architecture is the most immediate, expressive and lasting art to ever record the human condition. We are what we build; stone and steel do not lie. But there has been a radical change in the way we perceive and understand this physical reality. Surrogate experience and synthetic settings have become the preferred American way of life.
>
> (Huxtable 1997: 1)

In joining theatre, or "playacting," to the "disengagement from reality" that Las Vegas exemplifies, Huxtable (1997) places herself within a long line of anti-theatrical polemics.[2] Las Vegas is quite obviously and unabashedly a city where the grandness of architecture is turned into a temporality akin to the canvas flats or rear projections of the theatre: fleeting environments that refuse to testify to permanence or an enduring original. It invites its visitors to revel in this theatricality, to feel themselves to be changeable, teasing the real with its opposite, resisting the real that calls them back to ordinary lives.

But the far more critical problem with Las Vegas is not that people obviously love its theatrical fakery. There is a different point of view from which to challenge the staging of the really made-up in Las Vegas, a point of view which has nothing to do with traditional distrust of the theatre. It has to do instead with seeing how the pleasure we take in performed invention in Las Vegas is bound up, as it is in other brandscapes, with the commodity form and with articulations of power. This means that we have to take the theatricality of Las Vegas seriously, neither vilifying it in some entrenched classicist vein, nor treating it lightly as harmless, if tacky, theatrical fun.

At least Huxtable takes the effects of playing in a theatrical indeterminacy between the real and the fake seriously. She seems to believe that Las Vegas' undoing of the real will have deleterious historical, cultural and social effects. She doesn't treat it as fantasy, the term customarily used for a temporary experience with no lasting or real impact. Fantasy is perceived as just an escape, a short, embodied moment of otherness, with return to the real inevitable. It is as if the imagination doesn't produce real consequences. Huxtable (1997) is right, for her part, to sense that something serious is afoot in the fantastical synthetics of Las Vegas.

Arjun Appadurai (1990) admonishes us that we musn't any longer think of fantasy as "mere fantasy," or "simple escape," but must instead begin to think of it as part of a social field which he calls the imagination. It's through the imagination that people both act and are acted upon. The imagination, perhaps especially as it takes embodied, mimetic forms, can no longer be thought of as merely the idiosyncratic property of individuals but must rather be regarded as one of the places where power is organized, structured, and distributed. The imagination becomes a "productive capacity" (Hardt and Negri 2000: 213) through which we reproduce power.

The image, the imagined, the imaginary – these are all terms
that direct us to something critical and new in global cultural
processes. *the imagination as social practice.* No longer mere fantasy
(opium for the masses whose real work is elsewhere), no longer
simple escape (from a world defined principally by more
concrete purposes and structures), no longer elite pastime (thus
not relevant to the lives of ordinary people), and no longer
mere contemplation (irrelevant for new forms of desire and
subjectivity), the imagination has become an organized field
of social practices, a form of work (in the sense of both labor
and culturally organized practice), and a form of negotiation
between sites of agency (individuals) and globally defined fields
of possibility. This unleashing of the imagination links the play
of pastiche (in some settings) to the terror and coercion of
states and their competitors. The imagination is now central
to all forms of agency, is itself a social fact, and is the key
component of the new global order.

(Appadurai 1990: 31)

In this excerpt, Appadurai draws quite close to a sense of Hardt
and Negri's conception of immaterial labor in a "society of control"
in which power reaches deep into all aspects of social life, making
every part of that life one of its productive fields. A key form of
that immaterial labor, I believe, is our labor to bring forth into
embodiment as necessary and life-fulfilling the meanings embedded
in corporate contexts, or contexts otherwise constitutive of power.
Imagination, including maybe most importantly, embodied enactment, is not a means to escape social structures, but is instead a
primary resource through which those structures can be maintained or produced.

This chapter will be built around an ancient metaphor that has
for a long time been a means by which performance (or the
embodied imagination) has been understood to have very real
social effects, and to be absolutely caught up in formations of
power. I refer here to the theatrum mundi, or the idea that all
the world is a stage. In its historical form, the theatrum mundi
was used to make people understand their life as performance, an

imagined construction scripted and spectated by God. Life was thus placed within the field of the imagination, full of negotiations between what was real and what was not. Embodied enactment was the way that people labored to bring themselves forth in the correct form, the form mandated by power, a form saturated with power's meanings.

The Forum Shops resonates with the idea. The gods watch us move through the mall from their celestial viewpoint above the shops, and Bacchus invites us into enactment – initially as guests welcomed into a party designed by the gods and, later, as we shall see, as participants in a high-stake scenario involving the recovery of the city of Atlantis, lost on account of greed and ambition. Most people feeling themselves thus scripted will likely experience it as a moment of that "mere fantasy." But I wish to push on the metaphor of the theatrum mundi because to do so is a way to see our performance in the mall as something that does indeed have serious social consequences. At the Forum Shops, the theatrum mundi functions as one of Appadurai's organized fields of social practice: linking the really made up to the coercions of the market.

I'll argue that at the Forum Shops there is a shift, a surrogation, so that the place of God in the theatrum mundi is assumed by the commodity form. The script into which we are drafted at the mall serves to dress gambling and consumption in the costume of morality, and righteous independence from the degradations of greed and avarice. Just as the theatrum mundi traditionally negotiated the problems of agency (free will), greed, loss, ruin, and the imagination, here in the mall its reappearance does likewise, not to bring people under god's thumb, but to bring them under the commodity's.

We'll look more closely at the theatrum mundi trope, but first let's return to the mall, and to Bacchus, whose tone darkens. We're about to be absorbed into a play centered on the fall of Atlantis to the depths of the sea. Our immersion in the Atlantis script begins in the mall environment, taken as a whole. It's surreal, as if lost, a city that could not really exist. All the windows are illuminated (anachronistically) from within, as are the equally anachronistic street light fixtures. Overhead a sky filled with shifting, fluffy, white cumulous clouds stretches a concave blueness over the space. The city feels subterranean, drowned. There's the watery entryway, the ubiquitous fountains and sound of water, and the estranging juxtaposition of night and day. It's as if the place were an undersea palace from a fairy tale, down so deep that it has to be illuminated while overhead the cosmos still stretches itself. This totalizing environment seems to be designed to alter us sensorially, mimetically, to feel as if we are submerged in this unreal, watery depth.

This sensorium is brought into clear focus in an installation at the center of the mall, in the Roman Great Hall. It's a huge circular fish tank, ringed with benches, perhaps two and a half times as tall as an average person. It dwarfs the people around it, seeming almost to engulf them. It creates the sensation that we are simultaneously witnesses to and participants in this alluring oceanic world. Inside, rare, colorful, tropical fish swim among huge blocks of stone not unlike that used in the architecture of the mall. The blocks lie in careless heaps, clearly the remnants of some devastation. Great white statues in Roman-esque armor lie askew among these blocks, as if toppled from the heights. They look just like the statues in the mall would look if they fell. Stone columns, ceramic jugs, jewelry and other detritus from a ruined civilization are also drowned in the watery exhibit. This tank deepens the sense that we are in a surreal and unfamiliar world. We are no longer ourselves, people who belong to the white heat now long forgotten on the city streets outside. This is a fake world, a stage set, to which we nevertheless give ourselves over, spying on the remains of a destroyed world, a world unreachable at the bottom of the ocean.

Back at the "Fountain of the Gods" show, the music moves to an ominous key and the lights change to a darker tint. Having been invited into the wonders of pageantry (playacting), we are now introduced to the narrative or script which underpins the sensorial cues of the mall. The watery touches, the fishy ruins, are all part of an accumulating network of references to the myth of Atlantis. In this myth, originating with Plato, a utopian island city, originally given to Poseidon as his share of the world, sinks beneath the weight of the greed of his many descendants, all whom hope to gain the city's wealth for themselves. So, Bacchus warns, notwithstanding the pleasure and pageantry available in the mall:

> All is not well in the Forum shops. Greed and envy have
> brought down the city of Atlantis. But you, my dear guests,

will experience how the story of Atlantis continues through the forum of the great hall and perhaps by witnessing the downfall of the city of Atlantis, you will leave here a little wiser.

In this speech, the robot Bacchus does not exactly conflate the mall with Atlantis, but he implies that the two are connected. The downfall of Atlantis darkens the Forum mall. Unless, that is, shoppers get wise to the pitfalls of avarice. In a place dedicated to consumption, we are to learn to negotiate greed. He finishes by issuing us forth into our performance of his script: "Go forth, and enter the magic. I raise my goblet to wish you well on your journey."

The group of performers/consumers who have watched the show, myself among them, surge almost as one body down the corridor of the mall leading to the Roman Great Hall where the "Lost City of Atlantis" will play. Since the beginning of this show is timed, of course, in coordination with the end of the "Fountain of the Gods" show, there is time to shop along the way. The gods above the stores watch us move through the prescribed pattern, the avenues of the market. The group reassembles eagerly at the central fountain, starting about ten minutes before show time. We shove together into an audience so tight that it is hard to move. There is keen anticipation all around.

The huge fountain/stage is adjacent to the fish tank and its ruins. At rest, this stage appears simply as a large set of nonspecific, white, Romanesque statuary. But every hour there are voluminous clouds of fog, loud music, thunder and changing lights as this set of statuary sinks into the base/stage and a formidable audioanimatronic threesome rises, from the depths of the sea, in their place. The king, the father, sits high up, center stage, on a throne. Downstage of him on either side are his two children. The daughter is the queen of ice and the son is the prince of fire. These robots are fully costumed in richly decorated clothes, perhaps to signify their accumulation of wealth. The children begin a vicious battle over who will inherit the father's city – Atlantis. The two greedy sibling robots cry out to the audience asking for support. "Who will support me?" each screams. Spectators cry out in response, choosing sides: "I will!" "I will!" In the end, the king is overcome by his children's greed and dissonance and, raising his scepter, in a crack of thunder, smoke and water, takes his children and his city with him to the bottom of the ocean in a massive act of destruction. Atlantis is irreparably lost.

And yet, after all, Atlantis is not as irretrievable as it might seem. After the show, performers/consumers can buy their tickets to a virtual reality ride called "The Search for Atlantis." The entrance to the ride is just by the stage which, following the havoc, is restored to its neutrality. We've moved through the mall, from the "Fountain of the Gods" show to the Atlantis show as enjoined to do by Bacchus. The next step, following the climactic point at which Atlantis descends to the depths, is for us to perform, through the medium of virtual reality, a scenario in which we will be able to discover and retrieve the lost city.

An advertisement at the entrance to the ride reads: "Your mission from the Gods, should you choose to accept it, is to fly a hurtling chariot past crashing boulders and evil goblins to win the Race for Atlantis." The ride, creating the kinesthetic, bodily effect of being fully in the experience, hurtles participants through the depths of the ocean, a thrilling ride past threatening monsters, deep ocean crevasses, and other dangers, toward the lost city and its recovery.

We are the virtual heroes, rescuing the city, and ourselves, from the effects of greed, our paths scripted and spectated by god.

The theatrum mundi

Let's turn now for a quick look at the theatrum mundi trope to see how the scripted journey we take through the mall resonates with this historical construction of performance as a social field that organizes our willing embodiment. The theatrum mundi begins as a negotiation between the real and the fake that is joined to theology. It moves, by the Renaissance, to a secular formation in which the market displaces God as playwright and audience.

Plato is probably the earliest known philosopher to use the image of the theatrum mundi. True to his characteristic ambivalence toward representation, Plato argues that real life is the true drama and that actors' or tragedians' dramas are only falsifications of this more profound theatre. Nevertheless, he is responsible for introducing one of the first images of God as playwright.

The Roman Stoics also depended upon God as playwright, with life conceived as a performance, and nothing more. Being only performance, life could be undertaken dispassionately, with care that one's roles, as scripted by God, were played well so that the coherence on earth intended by God could materialize. Following the Stoics, the early Christians adopted the idea that life is a performance created, scripted, and watched by God. However, the trope began to shift with their idea of a life after death with God. Christians were to understand that the seductions of the earthly world were merely part of a performance, and therefore would jeopardize their true selves, which would be experienced after death in their life with God. St. Augustine (350–430), for example, writes that "For the whole life of temptation in the human race is a stage play; for it is said: Every man living is altogether vanity" (Christian 1987: 39). The devout person of the early Christian period thus remains detached from the earthly show. The only spectacle worthy of praise is the spectacle of Judgment Day and beyond, and people's days were to be spent in preparation for the witnessing of this spectacle. This view was articulated especially by Tertullian:

> The spectacle of life is now purely transcendental. . . . it is the spectacle of redemption, the spectacle of the Last Judgment, the spectacle of Christ crucified. The stage of the world has collapsed and the stage of the sky has opened up before the suffering Christian.
>
> (Christian 1987: 37)

By means of the theatrum mundi then, the Stoic and early Christian alike are positioned within theologies that control and coerce his relation to earthly life and the nature of his selfhood.

After the early Christian period, the trope fell into disuse for much of the Middle Ages. It resurfaced in the fifteenth century in a radically different form. The source of the new view was a body of writing from the middle of the second century, called the Corpus Hermeticum, which was rediscovered, translated and circulated throughout the Renaissance. Most significantly, the Hermetic angle on the theatrum mundi endowed human beings with a creative ability akin to God's, and expressed in a protean capacity to play many different roles. According to the Hermetic position: "Man has been plucked from the hierarchical ladder of the Great Chain of Being and has been given an infinite possibility of roles to play as a microcosm of the divinely created universe" (Christian 1987: 79).

Pico della Mirandola follows suit in his "Oration on the Dignity of Man," where God expects that humans will use the agency he's given them to make their own choices about what or who they wish to become, and what parts they wish to play on life's stage. In this excerpt from his Oration, God is speaking to Man:

> We have made thee neither of heaven nor of earth, neither mortal nor immortal, so that with freedom of choice and with honor, as though the maker and molder of thyself, thou mayest fashion thyself in whatever shape thou shalt prefer.
>
> (Christian 1987: 80)

In Juan-Luis Vives' *The Fable about Man* (1518), Juno asks Jupiter to stage a play with new characters as a birthday gift to her. Jupiter brings forth the whole world as a stage. Jupiter himself is director (again, not unlike our Bacchus), commanding the appearance of each actor and ordering each to strictly adhere to his direction. But then the audience of gods notices how much the actors resemble them. Like them, the humans seem to be able to assume any shape, even a god's. One actor even impersonates Jupiter himself and does it so successfully that the other gods, tricked, are upset that Jupiter has lowered himself to acting. Man, the actor, is led to the auditorium where he takes his place as one of the gods while the gods marvel at his costume – which is the five senses through which he achieves his protean enactments.

In these Renaissance views of the theatrum mundi, the ontological status of the human being is indeterminate. Humans are fluid beings who have the agency to shape themselves according to their own desires. The shift in the trope accompanies, not accidentally, the seismic shifts from feudalism to capitalism. If the changes in ideas of humans' theatrical being begin to free people from the coercions of the church, the same changes make them ready for the coercions of the market. Here the history of the theatrum mundi begins to connect to the pleasure we take in trying on the shapes, or performing the scripts, that tie us to the market. The Forum Shops' audioanimatronic Bacchus bears much more resemblance to the God of Mirandola's "Oration" than to the God of the early Christian period. The world, in this Renaissance moment, becomes a wide open field where humans adopt for themselves multiple faces. Far from being a sin against God, the path to evil, this proteanism is an image of God's own creativity, a shape shifting performance that God very much enjoys. Our Bacchus, a performer himself, invites us into our parts.

The emergent capitalist market in which the theatrum mundi reemerged is a market, as Jean-Christophe Agnew describes, where the product of labor floated into the market independent of its producer. It was translated into that abstract and faceless form of equivalence – money – whose value was realized by another faceless and unknown individual. To make these exchanges, to sell their labor, people began to have to think of themselves as changeable identities, faces manufactured according to the necessities of the particular transaction at hand. The trope of the theatrum mundi, in its Renaissance inflection, offered performance as the model according to which to style selfhood in a society where traditional structures of identity and meaning were ceasing to have coherence or validity. It configures a performing self, a constructed self, whose acting is scripted not by God but by the imperatives of the market. We shall see how this becomes true of our Bacchus and the narrative into which we are drawn. Agnew says:

> The same theatrical metaphor that had for so long served churchmen to wean the faithful from their attachments to the secular world became over time a symbolic representation of attachments and moorings already lost, and lost not through some putatively divine intervention in the world or some voluntary, personal withdrawal from the world, but rather through the radically defamiliarizing effects of commodity exchange. What made the theatrical metaphor so resilient was no doubt its capacity to evoke the sense of a lived abstraction of distinctively human contrivance, a "second nature" whose facticity was best represented by a theater that was itself increasingly detached from any ritual relation to God.
>
> (Agnew 1986: 16)

For Agnew, retrieving the trope from its relative obscurity is a way to position the physiognomic effects of the market, the way that it structures meaning and perception, at the center of economic and cultural analysis. Performance is a means to move through suppositions about the market's supposed neutrality to a study of its affective structures and responses: the anxieties, problems and ruptures initiated by the commodity form and the money form.

This is exactly what I want the trope to do here. At the Forum Shops, it is both a conceptual model by which to think about our relation to the market and a materialized three-dimensional space in which to encounter the way that the commodity organizes our perceptions. The way that the market organizes our performance in this theatrum mundi is initiated by processes of surrogation.

Surrogation: how the market slips in to this theatrum mundi

It is not exactly accurate to say that in the Forum Shops our performances are watched over by gods. They are, rather, watched over by audioanimatronic figures that have stepped into the place of gods, performing as gods.

According to Joseph Roach (1996), surrogation may be the most defining process involved in performance. He remarks that different descriptions of the hard to define act of performance all "commonly assume that performance offers a substitute for something else that preexists it. Performance, in other words, stands in for an elusive entity that it is not but that it must vainly aspire both to embody and replace" (Roach 1996: 3). Performances, Roach says, create effigies, a word he uses especially in its verb form. In this form, effigy, almost like performance itself, is the act of manifesting, bringing into being something that was absent. This is especially the case in the sense of recovering something from the past. It is not so much the fabricated image of someone, a thing, as it is a "set of actions that hold open a place in memory" (Roach 1996: 36). The function of the effigy is to provide societies with a way to perpetuate themselves because the effigy holds open this "place in memory" into which a number of surrogates, stand-ins for the original, can step.

At the Forum Shops, the audioanimatronic figures of Bacchus, Venus and Apollo in the "Fountain of the Gods" show are, obviously, surrogates for gods and, specifically, for Roman gods of pleasure. The choice of Rome is shrewdly tactical on the part of its designers for a number of reasons. The theatrical culture of Rome was the last significant exploration of the meanings of performance prior to the Christian censorship and denunciation of theatre. In their amphitheatres and pantomimes, the Romans made high spectacle of the real being made into performance and then back into the real.

Along with the evocation of the pre-Christian pleasures of performance and "pageantry," the choice of Rome as the prototype for Caesar's Palace and the Forum Shops also bypasses Christian anti-corporeal philosophy in favor of a model which legitimizes the pleasures of the body, its passions, and its drive to be sated.[3] In other words, it legitimizes consumption, the rush to the stores and the slot machines. Any period after the Roman is complicated by the presence of Christianity and the echo of its asceticism, its reminders of the poor and the oppressed. The walls of Caesar's Palace are, so to speak, padded by the choice of Rome as its theme. We'll see that the Atlantis script smoothes the path for gambling and shopping but so does the immersion in Rome. Performers/consumers/gamblers are protected from the whisperings of the guilty conscience (and the anti-theatricality) of the Christian tradition, the guilty whispers which most likely saturate their daily lives far away from the simulations of Las Vegas.

There is another important surrogation afoot. Unlike live actors and like the commodity, the performances by the robots are things that recur in the same way each time. They can be endlessly reperformed, without deviation, just as the commodity is churned out of the assembly line, each identical to the last. Unlike any kind of live performance, every aspect of this performance is repeated in its exact form every half hour. Surrogates are never exactly the thing they stand in for and the robotic performances are not exactly the commodity. However, they draw ontologically close to the commodity in their absolute reproducibility: they stand in for commodity, and keep its place in memory.

The robots are the point at which two surrogations converge: commodity and divinity. In the process, the Roman gods, the watchers of the theatrum mundi, slide into the commodity form. Through the surrogation of the robot, the gods become, not exactly a commodity, but like a commodity. It's this commodity/god who scripts our actions in the mall.

Because of its reproducibility, the robot's performance is also a template imposed on performance. It is a paradox that this little god of the theatre and of altered states, god of Dionysian trance and excess, who drafts us into the "wonders of pageantry," is subject to the limitations of his programming, from which his motion cannot deviate. The script into which he drafts us is also a template; it's a performance that moves us down the identical traffic flow of the mall each time, to be part of another performance which occurs in exactly the same way each time, to move into the hollow core of another commodity, the virtual reality ride, which is also characterized by deadly reproducibility.

The robotic show is a way to stamp performance with a template that disciplines the excess performance potentially unleashes. The template controls any way in which our protean capacities might slip us out of the coordinates of power. As in the traditional theatrum mundi, performance is evoked only to be coerced. As in the theatrum mundi that emerged in the Renaissance, our play-acting is induced in order to position us in the market as playable selves. Our paths are managed, in and through the stores and restaurants of the mall, through the Atlantis script, and ultimately into the casino. And somehow, the experience is keenly pleasurable. Somehow we take pleasure not only in the performance that the commodity/god scripts for us, but also in the template through which it makes it appearance and into which it shapes ours.

Philip Auslander (1999) gets at something like this template with the concept of franchised performance. He gives as examples interactive performances like *Tamara* and *Tony and Tina's Wedding*; "Producers of the genre known as 'interactive plays' envision live performances as franchisable commodities" (Auslander 1999: 47). Elinor Fuchs (1996), in a similar vein, recounts her conversation with Barrie Wexler, the producer of *Tamara*, who franchises rather than leases the show worldwide in order to ensure that the product will be reproduced in exact detail every time. He thinks of himself as a retailer and has modeled his operation on "McDonald's, the airline industry, the insurance business, and the superstores, like IKEA and Home Depot" (Fuchs 1996: 142). Fuchs provides a description of watching *Tony and Tina's Wedding*, which is a sensorial guide to what happens to performers/consumers who are scripted into the *Tony and Tina* franchise.

> Here actors deliberately do not exert their former claims to characterological authenticity . . .; rather, they proclaim their inauthenticity, their artificiality, exhibiting themselves as a series of ever-changing, and not necessarily connected, impressions and surfaces. The actors in effect invite me to model myself as a series of reflecting surfaces, moving in and out of the changing environment in a playful, half-immersed, half-detached state of simulacrity, an instant, every-shifting simulation in which I "try on" the physical and imaginative

conditions imposed by the surrounding space. The heavy
burden of "auracity" has been lifted not only from the actors
but from me as well. I am pleasantly suspended in what might
be thought of as authentic artificiality.

(Fuchs 1996: 140)

In Fuch's description, the performers/consumers can surrender
themselves to the freedom of the reproduction, appear as one of
the many surfaces of the franchise, the template, with no need to
refer to an auratic human self. The sensation of the really made
up, trying on this "authentic artificiality," is one of heightened
pleasure, and yet the performance is one that occurs in the same
form, like a McDonald's, in many different locations. Each of these
pleasurable immersions in the really made up is stamped by a
template into a recognizable and repeatable pattern. The same is
true of the Forum Shops. Each time the performance of the group
of performers/consumers is scripted, that performance is simultaneously a template.

Why is it that we are so drawn to the robot, the commodity/
god? Why do we take pleasure in surrendering to the template,
the script, the ways by which we are fixed into the coordinates of
the commodity? We can conjecture that it has to do with what
Walter Benjamin called our "empathy with the commodity"
(Benjamin 1999: 375).

Benjamin theorized that we have come to feel more akin to the
commodity than to other human beings. This kinship is produced
by the relations of production and exchange. The specificities of
my labor are subsumed into abstracted units of measurement by
which my labor is valued, and this becomes the exchange value
of the commodity. What I am, what I do, is embedded in the
commodity. In a sense, then, my singularity disappears, absorbed
into its price, or exchange value. The same is true of others.
Humans circulate, including through their meetings with others,
in terms of this generalized value – just as commodities meet
each other in the market as units of value from which any residual
valuation according to specific use or need has disappeared.
Benjamin says:

It is only as commodity [and not as a thing of use – produced
by a person to meet his needs] that the thing has the effect
of alienating human beings from one another. It produces this

effect through its price [exchange value]. What is decisive is the empathy with the exchange value of the commodity, with its equalizing substrate.

(Benjamin 1999: 386)

We are enveloped in a world where all things, including ourselves, circulate according to a value determined by the market. We feel this world, and the commodities which are its clearest instantiation, to be the familiar world. The singular, vulnerable human being is a possibility whose claim on us is too demanding. The allures of the commodity are recognizable and pleasurable. We are tempted and do turn to the face of the Blackberry, or the Game Boy, away from the risk of encounter, of the almost certainly disorienting experience of recognizing, face to face, the astounding vulnerability of the human person. Our affinities, more and more, are for the thing, and for humans appearing in thing like forms.

Benjamin, watching the prostitutes of Paris, so numerous that they appeared identical, like the commodity in their replicated forms, wrote that, "love for the prostitute is the apotheosis of empathy with the commodity" (Benjamin 1999: 375). The film actor, as opposed to the live one, struck Benjamin in a similar way. In the figure of this actor, the human face, human experience, circulates explicitly as commodity. In the film actor, the human appears, but is encased, made product, invulnerable. We love to fall under its spell. We do fall under its spell. The actor himself, Benjamin says, is cognizant that his image, infinitely replicable, has become a transportable thing that will come before "the consumers who constitute the market" (Benjamin 1968: 231). Benjamin says that as live performance is displaced, the film industry "preserves not the unique aura of the person but the 'spell of the personality,' the phony spell of a commodity" (Benjamin 1968: 231).

The robot Bacchus seduces with the "phony spell of the commodity." But the creators of the Forum Shops have simultaneously preserved a space for the possibilities of embodiment. The robot, closer to thing than to human, a performance that is decisively transportable and repeatable, is at the same time a three-dimensional embodied thing. His three-dimensionality, most importantly, makes the mall a stage, a *playing* space, the means by which our bodies are sucked in, playing as our own experience the mall's fiction. But our performance is initiated by the pleasure we take in and our affinity for this thing and his replicated gestures. Our own performance is determined and bounded as an aspect of this replication, our playing, too, repeatable. There is little of the always unexpected provocations of live (unrepeatable) performance, those flare-ups of human singularity to which we seem less and less drawn as we seek out, increasingly, franchised performances.[4] A live actor as Bacchus would introduce the problematic of the "unique aura of the person." The robot, surrogate for the commodity, introduces the pleasures of a three-dimensional, bodily engagement without interrupting or challenging the affinity we feel for that circulating thing, that phony spell. This may be, in the deep perceptual structuration by capital of our phenomenological being, why we enjoy the robots, and so enthusiastically undertake our scripted journey through the mall.

To sum up my points thus far: the mall is structured by the theatrum mundi in the sense that it summons the theatre and the power of its histrionic, kinesthetic forms of imaginative enactment. But it also contains and manages that power. It is thus a social field comprised of the embodied imagination, and having real, coercive effects. The problem is not, as in Ada Huxtable's (1997) critique, that the fake of the mall is undoing the lasting meanings of the real Rome. The problem is that the real fake or the really made up serves here as a medium through which the agendas of capital can find their way. Bacchus stands in for the commodity, making the commodity something that is itself theatrical, that summons theatricality. But the commodity form, as a template, as duplicate experience, simultaneously controls and shapes theatricality, so that the pleasures it offers are those of playing a range of faces operable in a commodity driven society, or in a particular brandscape – not the transformative promises of another, almost unimaginable, theatre of liberating identifications. The little Bacchus, leering with his cup, invites us into the festivities – wine, music, song and transformation. But, with each jolting, repeated instant of that invitation, he implicitly calls back his own character; Bacchic, transformative excess is disciplined by plastic, wires and computer chips on a timer. Our own experience in the mall is undertaken according to this model of theatricality or performance stamped into a repeated and repeatable experience. The protean embodiments of the theatre are deployed to script our experience into a series of franchised performances. As franchised performances, they will make the agendas of the god/commodity, in whom lurks the logic of capital accumulation, tangible, read-able, and knowable. In the next and final section, we will look more closely at those agendas.

The hollow commodity and the recovery of Atlantis

Benjamin, through his close study of the allegorical work of the nineteenth-century poet Charles Baudelaire, concluded that the allegory and the commodity share an important characteristic; each uses its form only as a shell into which a limitless series of meanings can be poured. Allegory takes an object, an image or a story, and empties it out so that what it may mean at any partic-ular time has little to do with the signifier. The corollary to this in the commodity is that it too is a signifier to which any number of arbitrary meanings can be assigned, in the form of prices (see Benjamin 1999: 22). Its value, again, is not in what it is (use-value), but is rather in what it is worth, based on arbitrary configura-tions of market determinates. This means that any one meaning can just as easily be replaced by another. Theodor Adorno described this arbitrariness as a hollow quality of commodities, which allows the commodity to pull into itself the longings of consumers: "The alienated objects become hollowed out and draw in meanings as ciphers. Subjectivity takes control of them by loading them with intentions of wish and anxiety" (Buck-Morss 1995: 182). The virtue of placing the commodity in an allegorical narrative and dressed in allegorical roles is that neither the commodity nor the allegorical form in which it appears is tied to any permanent meaning and so it can be continually responsive, as a "cipher," to that which most concerns and inspires consumers in a particular environment.

The Forum Shops is a great hollow cavity, as are the fiberglass bodies of the robots, as is the open body of the virtual reality ride. These literalize the mall as Adorno's hollow commodity. The meanings that this commodity has pulled into itself, "the wishes and anxieties," have to do with the casino environment. It is a tremendous feat of allegorical magic that the commodity comes to be regarded not as the source of anxiety, guilt, and greed, but as an ally in overcoming them. In an environment that is satur-ated with personal and financial ruin, through consumption, addiction, and loss, the hollow body of the commodity, in the form of a virtual ride, and made allegorical through the myth of Atlantis, is for sale as a weapon against these evils.

There is a second allegory in which the Forum Shops is costumed, a testament by the commodity to its own power. Benjamin thought that, despite its allegorical talents, the commodity inadvertently tells of its own impermanence as the dominant feature of social relations. Because the commodity becomes so quickly disposable and valueless, thrown off the minute the fashion for it has passed, it exemplifies the historical tendency to ruin. It is proof that no historical situation is permanent and thus that our social condition is always changeable.

At the Forum Shops, the second tale the commodity tells about itself refutes this notion of its historical transience. It tells an allegory of its own permanence. This allegory saturates the whole environment of the mall. Whereas Rome (and its ruins) could conceivably be used allegorically as a warning about the inevitable fall and disappearance of great civilizations, here Rome is handily returned, in a spiffy new, fake, and commodified form. The commodity collapses itself into Rome, or, rather, Rome's central marketplace, and, in this Las Vegas revival of that city's market, tells an allegory of its own return: it signifies that it is not dependent on history, not subject to disappearance and ruin. As a theatrical thing it can always take on new garments, new meaning, and return afresh.[5] The commodity can recoup Rome, in this theatrical fake form, and appropriate its meanings as a template for contemporary consumption driven performance. By virtue of the fact that it can try on any culture, any meanings, the commodity flaunts itself as an a priori form, a substratum of all things.

The robotic fountains also perform the continuity of the commodity through the spectacle of their inevitable and ongoing repetition, reiteration, and reproduction: every half hour the two identical sets of statuary come to life. The commodity will always, reliably, return. Every hour the statuary sinks into the floor of the Atlantis fountain and the robotic King of Atlantis and his son and daughter rise in their place. So, while they disappear under the waves during their performance of destruction, these robot commodities return: performances whose details have been calculated and designed to be repeated and invariable. It is not they who will disappear, but a culture of greed (Atlantis), to which the commodity does not belong and from which it distances itself through its eternal return.

In this feat of brandscaping, a shopping mall is turned into a three-dimensional theatrum mundi. In a feat of ironic calculation, the theatrum mundi is structured around an allegory of greed, the mall spatially organized so that the bodies of visitors travel the illustrative patterns of a script warning against it. At the same time it is designed as an entertainment that will draw ever-larger crowds to the mall and seduce those crowds into ever-increasing consumption.

This is the primary way that this particular theatrum mundi negotiates a place for power through performance: people come to Las Vegas fully aware of the dangers of their own greed, fully aware of the ways in which Las Vegas preys upon their hopes of getting more, much more, than they have. It is a city based on greed, utterly sophisticated in the means to produce greed and to thereby enrich its coffers from the pockets of people who are, thereby, frequently ruined. We began this chapter with Caesar's Palace architect Sarno's intention of distancing visitors from the everyday world whose concerns might put a break on their gambling. The Forum Shops are a spectacular negotiation of this paradox: the commodity is a theatrical thing, a slippery thing, pulling onto itself many identities, meanings, and costumes. In this mall, the commodity/god pulls onto itself the costume of the eternal form. In a consummately commodified environment, we are reassured that, through the commodity itself, the devastating effects of greed can be redressed, the effects of destruction repaired.

This is the way in which the theatrum mundi in the Forum Shops fixes us within the coordinates of power. By recognizing the moral degradation that caused the downfall of Atlantis, and by wishing to rescue it, we are reassured that we are in control of our own greed. We look to the commodity, to the very thing that is at every turn inducing avarice (for merchandise, food, and the metallic cascade of coins from the slot machine) to assuage our anxiety about how we are to manage our fears of loss and our own greed in a society that depends upon the production of both greed and continual loss.

Chapter 3

The Lion King, mimesis, and Disney's magical capitalism

An advert in the program for *The Lion King*, Julie Taymor's stage version of the original Disney film, which opened in November 1997 at the New Amsterdam Theatre in New York, reads: "Enjoy your audience with the King. And remember, even in the jungle, American Express helps you do more." What is so striking about this ad is not only its blatant construction of the mutually beneficial relationship between theatre and the market, but also that it places audience members bodily inside the fiction of the musical. They are not merely an audience watching the lion king Mufasa on a stage, they are inside the play, enjoying their audience with him. The market, in the form of American Express, has a clear commercial interest in encouraging consumers to slide from their actual location as spectators of a show to fictional participant in the stage drama, which, in this case, is a multimillion dollar commodity.

The Lion King and its relationship to the Disney store that was originally adjacent to it is a startling instance of a brandscape configuration in which we are encouraged to do far more than to buy a commodity, pay for our ticket and consume the show, or its spin-offs. The Disney brandscape is designed, rather, to compel us to merge into the commodity as its life force. It depends on the commodity's claim on the mimetic imagination of consumers: we desire to be bodily like the commodity. It waits for us to bring it to life.

Since *The Lion King* opened, however, Disney's fortunes have changed. In this chapter I consider primarily what I call Disney's magical capitalism as it emerged in the heyday of the Disney stores and in the huge success of *The Lion King*. But I also look briefly at the more recent turmoil and transition within the company that began at end of the 1990s and the beginning of the 2000s. This power struggle between Roy Disney and Michael Eisner reveals the extent to which the company has historically been invested in awakening the mimetic desire of consumers and wedding that desire to its products Roy Disney and his supporters remain insistent upon this magical capitalism, sure that Eisner's raw corporatism, which ignores the power of mimetic allure, will devastate the company.

Magical capitalism: mimesis and the Disney Corporation

I use the phrase magical capitalism because the word "magic" has been at the center of Disney's presentation of its products, forming the core of Disney's stranglehold on American culture. In evoking the word "magic," the Disney Corporation has long understood that it carries with it the connotation of mimesis, as a strange and wonderful human proclivity. With its iteration of magic, Disney has sutured mimesis to corporate imagination.

The kind of mimesis Disney seized on is that which, as Michael Taussig describes it, involves not only making a copy of a thing through an imitation of it, but also contact, "a palpable, sensuous, connection between the very body of the perceiver and the perceived" (Taussig 1993: 21). In mimesis there is a "radical displacement of self in sentience" (Taussig 1993: 39), that opens up for us the possibility an "ineffable plasticity in the face of the world and the world's forms and forms of life" (Taussig 1993: 34). The process of copy and contact, plasticity of form, makes "sympathetic magic" (Taussig 1993: 47). Through sympathetic magic the copy acquires the power of the original, shimmers with its energies.

The revolutionary potential of this mimesis is that the blurring of self and other can confound practices of domination. A mimetic world is a "spiritualized" one, with animals, plants and humans miming, becoming one another, giving the self away into an exchange with otherness that then comes full circle in a cycle analogous to that non-capitalist economy of the gift society.

In their 1944 book, *Dialectic of Enlightenment*, Max Horkheimer and Theodor Adorno argue that, since the Enlightenment, the mimetic world, with all the potentialities that Taussig (1993) describes, has been lost to us. We've been structured to understand ourselves instead as separate, boundaried subjectivities whose relationship to others, to nature, and to our own selves is to achieve a form of domination or ownership over them. They write that Enlightenment man imagines himself as an "invisible power . . . the very image in which man attains to the identity of self that cannot disappear through identification with another, but takes possession of itself once and for all as an impenetrable mask" (Horkheimer and Adorno 1972: 10).

Their contemporary, Walter Benjamin, however, was more optimistic. He theorized a resurgence of the mimetic faculty in modernity and saw it as a potentially radical way of being in the world. Writing in the early years of the twentieth century under the spell of new technologies, and in particular of film, he felt that these technologies had the capability to draw subject and object close to one another, our eye an organ which reaches deep into and touches an image. The technology allows us to touch the object as a way to know it, in the way that children learn by taking on the bodies or forms of what they wish to know. The shock of the image brought close, Benjamin thought, could reestablish "the connection between imagination and physical innervation that in bourgeois culture has been snapped apart" (Buck-Morss 1995: 270). Somatic knowing could be revolutionary energy.

In a sense, Benjamin was right; modernity and its new apparatus have been the source of a resurgence of mimesis. Both Taussig (1993) and Elin Diamond (1997), as just two examples, take him up on the challenge and work to apply mimesis to the cause of a progressive politics. But Disney, too, has taken up the resurgence of mimesis. Perhaps it might be more accurate to say that Disney was itself highly instrumental in provoking new mimetic faculties into operation. A review from *Time* magazine of a 1950s Disney nature documentary, *The Living Desert*, might as well be quoting Benjamin on the mimetic qualities of film technology. Richard Schickel says that: "*Time* saw what Disney was getting at – 'the sense that the camera can take an onlooker into the interior of a vital event, indeed into the pulse of the life-process itself'" (Schickel 1997: 288).

If Adorno and Horkheimer condemned the disenchanted world, so did Disney. Disney has long worked to ameliorate the effects of a world denuded of mimesis, drawing on a formulation of magic that is, ironically, very close to that of Taussig's, Horkheimer and Adorno's. But of course this has been in the interests of its own profit-making mastery of animal, human and imaginative life.

Disney has made "magic," or enchantment, into a shining feature of capitalism rather than its antidote. It has pioneered *as a corporate technique* the embodied experience of an interconnected, relational "plasticity of form," particularly but not exclusively for children.

To Benjamin's mind, children are exemplary in being unconfined by the accepted definitions for or forms of things. The boundaries between things break down as children produce similarities or correspondences between them. Their understanding of the world occurs through this "mimetic improvisation" in which "perception and active transformation are the two poles of [their] cognition" (Buck-Morss 1995: 264).

The Mickey Mouse clubs that Disney inaugurated in the 1930s are one of the first instances of the way that corporate, profit-driven intent was yoked to children's way of knowing, to their "perception and active transformation." It may even be that Disney's early experiments with children in this regard were the inspiration for the corporate investment in mimetic strategies for adults and children alike that has come to characterize contemporary brandscapes.

The clubs were designed to facilitate the merchandising of toys that were spin-offs of the animated films. Disney established strategic alliances with department stores like Bloomingdales. There Mickey and Minnie appeared, embodied and in the flesh for the first time, introducing Santa Claus to children and handing out toys. Simultaneously, movie theatres that showed Disney films began hosting the clubs. To become a member of the club, children would have had to have gone to one of the participating stores, (Bloomingdales or Kresges), to procure and fill out the necessary application. The lobby of the theatre where club members then met would typically be displaying Mickey merchandise for sale as well as giveaways. By the end of 1930 one hundred and fifty movie theatres across the country had Mickey Mouse clubs.

The clubs extended the embodiment of the cartoon characters in the department stores into the theatres, where members came for the Saturday matinee program that was simultaneously a club meeting and a mix of Mickey-related entertainments. Club members were usually dressed in the very popular Mickey and Minnie playsuits and greeted each other with a Mickey Mouse handshake saying, "Hi, Minnie!" or "Hi, Mickey!" (deCordova 1994: 211). The little Minnies or Mickeys were then ready for the rest of the meeting, which consisted of "the recitation of the

Mickey Mouse Club Creed, the singing of 'America,' a stageshow or contest, the Mickey Mouse Club Yell, the Mickey Mouse Club Song" (deCordova 1994: 207), and then the feature film for the day. Children were thus involved in a mimetic process whereby their relation to Disney occurs by joining themselves to a Disney character, becoming Mickey or Minnie, perception through transformation. But this process deviates from Benjamin's vision. If for him children's mimetic play opens up meanings, here the meanings of the Disney characters the children played were already foreclosed. By mimetically seizing upon Minnie or Mickey, a child was only activating or enlivening a commodity that was already circulating through the world, communicating the fictions generated by the Disney brand. The human is fashioned in the image of the commodity. The child is made to feel like the Disney character/commodity, to feel as it, to feel for it, to feel empathetic connection with it. As Richard deCordova says of the Mickey Mouse Clubs, they were one of the earliest instances where having is conjoined to *being* (deCordova 1994: 211), possession linked to its opposite, mimetic immersion. Children, pulled into the emerging synergy of the market, induced to desire to have the Mickey Mouse doll, having seen Mickey Mouse movies, appear, themselves, *as* Mickey Mouse – and move into circulation on behalf of the brand's agenda.

The company continued to develop the ontological blur between human and Disney character, selling it as Disney "magic." Almost all of Disney's borrowed fairy stories tell of a world where the boundaries between what is imaginary and what is real collapse, where identity is fluid, transposable, and continually dissolving into otherness. People become animals, spirits speak from trees, and genies materialize from lamps. This interplay between forms, this fantastic fluidity, is the pull of this company, not only for children, but maybe even especially for many adults. The magical transformative subtext of the products is that there is a state of happiness that is other to that of known, daily life, the terrible grind of what most people feel to be a routinized, deadened and commodified society.[1] Many adults I talked to in the stores told me that wearing the Disney clothes, or some kind of Disney insignia, made them feel happy and/or brought back memories of a happy childhood. A clerk in one Disney store told me that a childhood lived in close association with the characters was happy because it was about fantasy. For this clerk, the opportunity to be a "cast member" in the store was a chance to recuperate that remembered magic.[2]

As a return to childhood, the products are a passage backward to a place and time when children were absorbed into these fictions as the very stuff of life, a time before the disenchantment of the adult world. In the following passage, Walt Disney himself clearly sets up the sense of an enchanted (mimetic) world that comes before, and is preferable to, this disenchanted one. The memory substance that is Mickey belongs to a prior, "primitive," world to which the Disney product gives us access. Mickey is our path backward to the enchanted world and also the substance that fills us when we get there.

> The Mickey audience is made up of parts of people; of that deathless, precious, ageless, absolutely primitive remnant of something in every world-wracked human being which makes us play with children's toys and laugh without self-consciousness at silly things, and sing in bathtubs, and dream and believe that our babies are uniquely beautiful. You know . . . the Mickey in us.
>
> (Schickel 1997: 158)

The appeal of the Magical Kingdoms (Disney Land and World), worlds set apart, is that within their borders people can be reabsorbed into a world of (supposedly) child-like perception, cognition and play. In this description from a Disney website, an adult indulges in the mimetic correspondences that Benjamin describes in the play of children. Everything in her field of vision is like, becomes, Mickey as she anticipates, feverishly, her trip to Disney World.

> Gwen and I leave for Disney World tomorrow morning. I can't explain it, but I get butterflies in my stomach at the thought of the trip, and I keep seeing shapes of Mickey Mouse in the most ordinary objects in my office, at home, even while sitting in traffic. Why, there's one stoplight that has cable in a circle on both sides of the light. The red light is Mickey's head; the circular cable, his ears . . . I follow the Mouse, because he represents quality, innocence and hope . . . I am part of his family.
>
> (http://www.dannhazel.com)

The brand new Disney theme stores that opened in New York City in the 1990s became an extension of this magical destination. They were venues that underscored the promise to consumers that they might be mimetically (magically) incorporated into or as Disney characters. Each store overtly underscored this connection with the placement of a large film screen at the center of the children's costume section that showed scenes from the parks. There were the Disney characters, humans dressed in the full body costumes whose limp playsuit form, awaiting the enlivening effects of a child's body, hung in endlessly replicated versions all around.

The stores were really clothes, or rather, costume stores. Unlike some other brandscapes studied in this book, there is no attempt to background the commodities in the store in favor of a more comprehensive brand message. At the Disney stores, the goods *were* the message. It was through the goods that the mimetic play transpired, the journey to the enchanted world. Every design element, and every bit of packaging, intensified the transformative suggestion of the playsuit, or even of the denim skirt for women, or the tie for men, slathered in colorful Disney characters.

As I've mentioned in the introduction, the first store to open, in the Staten Island Mall in 1995, featured a strange installation above our heads just inside the entrance. There was Donald Duck with a cartoon character film crew. He sat among a three-dimensional cartoon rendition of all the apparatus for making movies: a crane, a tracking system and movie lights. The clapper board identified the movie being made as "Movie Magic-Backstage Antics, Director: Mickey." Donald, the cinematographer, was aiming an old-time film camera at shoppers as they came into the store. Minnie Mouse cranked the film through the camera from behind him and out the images rolled, on the film negative curling in and through the airspace above the store. Donald's holding on to his hat, oh boy! His legs swing up, whooping, he's delighted with the results; we were no longer ourselves. In our passage through the Disney camera, we were, as Peter Quince in *A Midsummer Night's Dream* says of Bottom, "translated." On the negative were the silhouetted forms of the Disney characters we became: Minnie, Mickey, Pluto, Dumbo. It was as if we could in this way encounter, from the moment we stepped foot in the store, "the Mickey in us."

The two stores that subsequently opened in Manhattan were, like this first one, crowded with products whose packaging dripped with promises of "magical" transformation into "being" something different from what you are. Everywhere textual commentary extended the products as an invitation to an interchangeability of forms, to enactment. During the craze for the movie *Pocahontas*, the child was offered the chance, through playing with the toy, to "become a real Indian chief," "live as," or "experience just like" Pocahontas, or John Smith. I watched a little girl trying on a Snow White dress. We were being watched over by Mickey, who stood on a shelf over our heads, costumed in his role as the Sorcerer's Apprentice from *Fantasia*. He was looking directly down at us, book of spells opened, wand raised, facilitating magical becomings. I asked the girl why she wanted to wear the costume and she said, "To try and try and try to be a princess."

In the next section, we'll see how the mimesis that Disney encourages is directed toward making the Disney product seem to live – how we, absorbed into it, become the source of its animation.

Historical echoes

Subjectivity and the commodity: a French farce from 1464

Early in the history of capital, in 1464, an important play text, *Maistre Pierre Pathelin* introduced the idea that the emerging market and theatrical, mimetic play will draw phenomenologically close to one another. Its principal character is a master of the market, negotiating its slippery valuations with his own slips into multiple personas.

In the play, Pierre Pathelin, a trickster character who lives solely by his deceit, decides that he needs cloth so that he and his wife, Guillemette, can have new coats. Of course, they have not a penny to their name, so Pathelin thinks up a scheme by which he'll outwit the cloth merchant. He goes to the merchant's shop, cajoles the man with flattery, and invents for himself an identity by which he and the merchant share familial and business kinships from the past. Pierre Pathelin fingers the goods in the clothier's shop, admiring the colors of the fabrics, a historically new panoply of choice. Matching the display of commodities which the clothier hopes to sell, Pathelin in effect responds in kind by displaying a "false" self which he hopes the clothier will "buy."

Pathelin convinces the merchant to let him have two bolts of the very best fabric on credit, and further convinces him to let him take the fabric away with him. Because he has said that he has left his money at home, he invites the merchant to come collect the money and stay for a dinner of roast goose. Of course, there's not a crumb of food or a single cent at Pathelin's house. In the face of this offer, which he accepts, the merchant meets Pathelin with a dissimulation of his own, overcharging Pathelin for the goods. Blustering with fake altruism, he offers to give the cloth to Pathelin for a special rate of only 24 sous. When Pathelin has left, with the bolt under his arm, he feels that he's gotten the better of his customer, and congratulates himself on his act: "Well, there's no buyer so clever that he won't find a seller who can outwit him. That would-be trickster was stupid enough to pay 24 sous a yard for cloth that's not even worth 20!" (Maddox 1984: 178).

Jean-Christophe Agnew (1986) contextualizes the emergence of the "mobile" or "trickster" self in the early modern transition to a form of market exchange that is newly depersonalized by the abstract form of money, and that uproots earlier forms of identity. He says:

> What image of the individual could take adequate measure of a self no longer, or at least not fully, authorized within the traditional religious, familial, or class frame? And if such conventions, devices, and imagery were indeed available, where might they develop freely enough to coalesce into an intelligible, formal analogue of the increasingly fugitive and abstract social relations of a burgeoning market society? Where else, we might ask, but the theatre? . . . The professional theatre of the English Renaissance became in effect a "physiognomic metaphor" for the mobile and polymorphous features of the market.
>
> (Agnew 1986: 10, 11)

Pierre Pathelin is an excellent early example of Agnew's point. The play is a laboratory exploring the consequences of the performance of serial selves, and of negotiating a system in which others are dissimulating also. It's built around trans- actions that, unsecured by traditional social placements or loyalties or legislation, are performed as simulations, enact- ments calculated to ensure gain.

When the merchant arrives for his goose dinner and the money he is owed, he is greeted by a distraught Guillemette. Pierre, she says, is dying, raving on his death bed, a lunatic. (Pierre, the master performer, calls on his knowledge of many different dialects to enact convincing lunacy.) Guillemette, whose performance has been scripted in advance by Pathelin, gradually manages to convince the befuddled merchant that he could not possibly have sold Pierre any cloth. After all, she argues, Pierre has been here, dying, the whole time. The merchant only overcomes his suspicions that they are tricking him when he hears for himself the ravings of the bedridden lunatic.

Against the solid, inert subjectivity of the merchant, Pathelin puts the market into motion for his own profit. The merchant finds himself bettered in a game of appearances and fictions. He feels vertiginous:

The clothier (leaving the house):   By the gracious Virgin, I'm more confused now than ever. The Devil, in his shape, took my cloth to tempt me. (Crosses himself.) *Benedicite*, may he leave me in peace. But since that's the way it is, I give the cloth, in God's name, to whoever took it. *(He exits)*

Pathelin (getting up, to Guillemette):   Now then, didn't I instruct you well? There he goes, the gullible simpleton. Now he's really got some confused ideas under that bonnet of his. I bet he'll have nightmares when he goes to bed tonight.

Guillemette: We really put him in his place. Didn't I play my part well?

Pathelin: By God, you played it to perfection. Now at least we have enough cloth to make some clothes.

(Maddox 1984: 190)

The ironic twist that shapes the final third of the play comes when the shepherd who cares for the merchant's sheep is introduced. He's received a court summons for the disappearance of many of those animals. He comes to Pierre Pathelin to ask Pathelin to be his lawyer, saying he'll pay him well. He confesses that he did in fact kill the sheep, though he told the clothier that they'd died of disease. What's more, he ate the sheep. Paid too little to survive, he subverted the merchant's chain of capital accumulation, literally ingesting the would-be commodity, asserting its use-value as food and subsistence.

Pathelin agrees to take the case, not knowing that this shepherd's employer and the cloth merchant are one and the same. Pathelin tells the shepherd to pretend to be slow-witted when questioned in court. He is to act as if he thinks he is talking to his sheep and therefore will only say "Baaa." The action of the play then shifts to the courtroom. Once there, the clothier of course recognizes Pathelin, and is enraged that Pathelin had duped him with the deathbed act. The surprised but quick-witted "master deceiver" Pathelin slips out from under all the merchant's attempts to verify his identity by unraveling all the merchant's statements through a maddening wordplay. The merchant becomes increasingly befuddled, his lack of market finesse fully revealed as, under Pathelin's influence, he keeps confusing his commodities: his sheep, the wool from his sheep, and his cloth. The more the angry merchant tries to pin down Pathelin's identity, the more foolish he looks.

The clothier: Do you think I'm an imbecile? It was you in person; you, yourself, and nobody but you. Your voice proves it and don't think it doesn't.

Pathelin: Me, myself and I? No, it wasn't, I swear. Get that out of your head.

[. . .]

The clothier: I'll renounce St. Peter if it wasn't you – you and nobody else. I know that to be absolutely true.

Pathelin: Well don't you believe it, because it positively wasn't me. I never took a yard or even half a yard of cloth from you. I don't have that kind of reputation.

The clothier: Damn it all, I'm going to go back to your house to see if you're there. We won't have to squabble here any more if I find you there.

(Maddox 1984: 1998)

In the meantime, during the trial, the shepherd has persisted in his baaas, speaking as the sheep commodity that he's eaten up. It is a blackly humorous version of absorbing commodities as the self, becoming like them. By so doing, he eventually wins his case against the merchant – his is the superior command of performance. In the final twist in this drama of market space performance, he continues to respond only with "baaa" even after the "show" is over. Pathelin congratulates him on a part well played and asks for his fee; it seems that even Pathelin expects that market performances have boundaries and that participants will return to the real. However, the shepherd sticks to his act.

The shepherd: Baa!
Pathelin: Is this the only pay I'll get? Who do you think you're playing games with? I was taking such pride in your performance; now really make me proud of you.
The shepherd: Baa!
Pathelin: Are you trying to pull the wool over my eyes? God's curse! Have I lived so long that a shepherd, a sheep in human clothing, a churlish knave can make a fool of me?
The shepherd: Baa!

(Maddox 1984: 199)

The play opens a vertiginous space where "truth," or what is real, is impossible to ascertain, a market space built on serial representations of self, read through acts of exchange. The clothier's characteristic misrepresentations of his retail and labor practices, and Pathelin's and the shepherd's facile performances obfuscate the very idea of identity and truth. Through these protean constructions of self, realized and given shape through interactions centered on buying and selling, the person draws ontologically closer to the commodity, whose value is likewise realized through acts of exchange in the space of the market. Performances, by both humans and commodities, must be serial, mutable, improvisatory. They are unhinged from inner worth or self-hood (humans) or use-value (commodities) since the market levels all products (humans and commodities) to a value determined by exchange, a value continually in flux. In the play, the shepherd is the only character who truly triumphs in the emergent market economy described by the play. He triumphs because he realizes the ontological closeness in the market between human and commodity (himself and the sheep he's eaten), and performs that relation in an ongoing and adaptable way. Exceeding even Pathelin in this, he is without need for recourse to any underlying human truth of self. The play makes a space for early moderns to experience the phenomenological closeness of the human to the market, playing with the way that persons in the market are like, and are encouraged to see themselves as, commodities.

Commodity fetishism: the store, the theme parks

The girl enacts, or becomes, or feels her likeness to Snow White, the woman sees Mickey in the traffic signal. In so doing they are making Snow White, or Mickey, into a commodity fetish; that is, Disney's organization of our mimetic play is such that our energies give the commodity what appears to be a life of its own.

One particular advertisement has become emblematic for me of corporate strategies through which the bodies of consumers become the source of a commodity's "life." One of the billboards dominating "the new Times Square" in 1998 advertised Disney's across-the-street-competitor, the Warner Brothers store. In the ad, the head of Tweety Bird filled the billboard on one side and, on the other side, a young girl wore a shirt emblazoned with the head of Tweety Bird. Above the shirt her face mimicked the expression that Tweety Bird characteristically wears. It was as if by costuming herself as, or becoming like Tweety Bird, she was infused with the life of Tweety Bird, who is, after all, a commodity. Her expression was the expressiveness of the commodity. The words "show your character" were written on a blank blue area between the two images. The ad played on the meanings of character as both the unique properties belonging to the individual, and a persona that is adopted through theatrical play. Inside the store which, like the Disney store, is now closed, the advertisement and its message was repeated everywhere with slightly different images. For instance, a girl "shows her character" by wearing a baseball cap which was decorated by Tweety Bird's eyes. The cap was pulled down so that instead of seeing her eyes, we saw Tweety Bird's eyes taking their place. The advertisement points to a chain of copy and contact, sympathetic magic. The girl touches and copies the commodity and absorbs its power. But the commodity is also copying her, the human, and acquiring her power. The girl and the commodity lose the boundaries that differentiate one from the other. The thing derives life from the human. The human derives life from the thing. The human is woven into the thing, and ultimately the thing appears the more lifelike of the two, as the fact of its dependency on the human fades from view.

It seems paradoxical that this kind of commodity fetishism functions as perhaps the only antidote to the disenchanted life. If humans are indeed mimetic creatures, why are we not drawn to experiment, "try on for size," forms of otherness that are not commodities? Why are we compelled to use our mimetic desire almost exclusively in conjunction with the commodity form?

In their writing on commodity fetishism, Jack Amariglio and Antonio Callari (1993) suggest that commodity fetishism is, in essence, creative. They speculate that Marx chose the figure of the fetish when he built his theory of the commodity precisely to draw upon the "mystery" of that image. Marx's use of the fetish

> suggests his own commitment to depicting the creative, innovative, and even fantastic process that creates the reality/myth of the "individual," the form of subjectivity that is continually shaped by and, in turn, shapes market relations. Even Marx's slight departure from a descriptive "scientific" language here precisely invites readers to enter into the continuing mystery, never fully resolvable, regarding the lack of ultimate closure of the individual and of the commodity relations this form of subjectivity makes possible.
>
> (Amariglio and Callari 1993: 203)

For Amariglio and Callari, the construction of subjectivity depends upon an unresolved openness in the consumer in tandem with the objective economic conditions that this ongoing process of subjectivity facilitates. That is, commodity fetishism functions in capitalist societies as precisely that process through which what Adorno calls the "impenetrable mask," or the rigid boundary circumscribing the Enlightenment self, is simultaneously rendered fluid.

Commodity fetishism is *the* mimetic medium. A given state of commodity relations produces the subject in a form that will be advantageous to the market in any given moment, but also ensures a commodity fetish in whose magical processes that subjectivity can be undone, unmade. The commodity, a creative vehicle, draws the human into itself.

At the Staten Island Disney store, I encountered a direct valorization of the commodity fetish, or its spectacular creative power exercised through the human. At the center of the store was an interactive touch screen that allowed me to choose to call up any of a selection of topics. Almost without exception Walt introduced the short film clips that I chose. In each introduction he said he was about to let me in on the secrets of Disney's "magic." On one of the ensuing film clips the voice-over crooned, "There's a lot of knowledge we have about how to entertain people by bringing *things* to life."

I chose a clip called "Audio-Animatronics." Walt appeared, saying that he wanted to show me how his lifelike creations, the audioanimatronic robots, were made. First, I saw the gelatinous, clear heads, filled with tubing and mechanisms, still in the workshop. The workings of these internal mechanisms were demonstrated, and then the skin was put on. The video cut to a now fully fashioned robotic "person," looking very much like an accurate facsimile of a human. He was sitting comfortably with his newspaper, on stage in a cozy, Americana living-room set, conversing with Walt. After a short while, the camera cut to a backstage area to view a human being strapped into a device that looked eerily like an electric chair. His head was in a metal cap, and his back and limbs were attached to metal rods. He was the source of the robot's "life," animating it through this full body remote control. Walt, chatting agreeably with the automata, never addressed the human who labored to make this "thing come to life."

Walt ostensibly defetishized his automata: he did show us the human labor that animated it. But he showed us only to show us how much less "magical" is the human. It's the human who looked thing-like. The human is frozen, trapped, routinized. By surrendering his energies to the commodity, those energies turn into something else, something freer, more expressive, more social and more life-like. Against the background of his effacement, the "magic" of Disney shimmers with its allure. We are meant to be awed by the power of the corporation to give life. We feel our own diminishment in the face of that creativity and so give ourselves over into making Simba's, or Snow White's, or Tweety Bird's liveliness.

The costumed workers in the Disney theme parks provide another remarkable example of this expenditure of human energies. At the theme parks, in contrast to Walt's demonstration of the robot, the human animating the commodity is specifically kept hidden. Jane Kuentz has done an alarming study that reveals the extent to which labor conditions in the theme parks enforce the total translation of the human into the copy that has appropriated its powers. I'll quote at some length from this study, done as part of a book by a collective called The Project on Disney (1995). Her work is based on interviews with employees and therefore useful to this argument for the first-hand insight it provides.

Corporate policy at the parks states that the park's obligation is to keep visitors' faith in "magic" alive. This means that nothing must interfere with the perception "guests" have that Disney commodities, as the embodied, full size characters who populate the park, are real. One worker says, "You're never to be seen in a costume without your head, *ever*. It was automatic dismissal" (The Project on Disney 1995: 136). When the characters travel to and from work, their costumes must be kept in black bags so that the costume is never seen as a costume, so that when it appears it will always be as a living body. One woman

> refused for an hour to acknowledge even that there were actual human people inside the Disney character costumes: "That's one of the things I really can't talk about. Not because I work there, but because it keeps it kind of sacred."
>
> (The Project on Disney 1995: 137)

Wearing the costumes comes at considerable risk to the vulnerable human bodies inside. The heads of the characters are so heavy and unwieldy that they have to be supported by metal braces that are custom designed for the bodies of their wearers. There is no peripheral vision. In the extreme Florida heat, workers stay out only twenty minutes at a time, after which they are required, heads still on, to repair to "backstage" areas. Even with this time restriction, many still vomit or pass out inside their character heads while "onstage," especially when, at the end of their twenty minute shift, they are unable to reach backstage before becoming ill. One man Kuentz interviewed describes his job, which is to drive around in a little cart and retrieve the unconscious bodies of passed-out cast members. He says:

> It's frightening because you can die on your own regurgitation when you can't keep out of it. I'll never forget Dumbo – it was coming out of the mouth during the parade. You have a little screen over the mouth. It was horrible.
>
> (The Project on Disney 1995: 136)

By and large, though, the employees of the theme park seem more than willing to endure these conditions. Disney hires people who specifically want to be part of the "magic," who apply for jobs hoping for the chance to become Mickey, or Minnie, or Snow White. According to Kuentz, workers are unfazed by their conditions of employment because their personal investments in the transformative powers of Disney run deep. One young woman says:

> I was very much an idealist about it, about it, about the job, and the whole Disney magic thing that they try to project to the public. I felt that all that magic and happiness was embodied in the character.
>
> (The Project on Disney 1995: 137)

Kuentz writes:

> The extent to which Disney workers seem actually to become their roles and thus embody magic and happiness – and this includes everyone, not just those in head costumes – is one of the most remarked and generally praised aspects of the park . . . Apparently this transformation to Disney product is what many of them want when they apply to the park in the first place.
>
> (The Project on Disney 1995: 137, 139)

Kuentz recounts this interview with "Ted":

> *Ted*: Let's say you were like Pluto, and you were the person in costume. See, I would never say that to anybody that

would write that in the paper, that there was somebody inside the costume. These kids come up and hug you and you sign the autographs and plus, you know, it's just something you have to experience, because you are the cartoon. You become Pluto. You have to experience it to understand.

JK: Is the "experience" the becoming Pluto or the interaction with the kids?

Ted: The interaction with the kids.

JK: I see.

Ted: As Pluto.

(The Project on Disney 1995: 134)

The commodity bodies enlivened by the disappeared human bodies that populate the theme park are echoed, albeit in a high art key, in Julie Taymor's production of *The Lion King*, which opened in New York in November 1997, to rave reviews as a "transporting" experience.

The primitive, modernist high art, and commodity fetishism in *The Lion King*

The production translates the flat, broad surfaces of the animated film into a marvel of mimetic fluidity, human into animal, into landscape, into plant, into animal. Like the film, it tells the story of a young lion, Simba, the son of the king, Mufasa. Simba is a mischievous cub who continually gets into trouble. His uncle, the villain Scar, takes advantage of the cub's disobedient curiosity to lead him astray. He offers to show him the elephant graveyard and, once there, sets his minions, the hyenas, in pursuit of Simba. Simba is lost and gets caught in a wildebeest stampede. His father finds out, goes to rescue him, and Scar kills Mufasa just as Mufasa is about to save Simba. In the second half, Simba, in the company of his two comic cohorts, Timon and Pumbaa, a meerkat and warthog, grows to young manhood. He is only occasionally haunted by the memory of the events of his childhood as he plays with his companions and sings "Hakuna Mutata" or "no worries." Eventually the young lioness Nala, his childhood playmate, who has been victimized by Scar, comes in search of him to bring him home to the starving Pridelands, desperate under Scar's rule. Simba comes back with her, defeats Scar, takes his rightful place as ruler of the Pridelands, and produces, with Nala, a new little lion heir, thus completing the reproductive circle, known in the production as "the circle of life."

Taymor has crafted each animal as a marvel of puppetry. Humans, whose own bodies are molded into service, animate full body carapaces to bring these characters "to life." For instance, the giraffes are people walking on all fours on stilts, with their faces just visible below the giraffe's neck and head, which are worn like an enormously elongated hat. The gazelles are mounted, in units of three, on the head and both arms of actors who are camouflaged in the shades and patterns of the animals.

Much of the beauty of *The Lion King* is in its mimetic transformations and correspondences, one thing becoming another, the human body glimpsed even as it disappears into the gazelle's leap. Taymor's marvelous scenic devices, which in a single sweep transform a group of humans into a savannah of waving grasses, certainly describe a relation to nature, as in Taussig's description of mimesis, that is "yielding" rather than dominating. Her human bodies, placed in an almost inextricable interplay with the animal bodies they inhabit, are displays of the protean self, "with multiple images of itself set in a natural environment whose animals, plants, and elements are spiritualized to the point where nature 'speaks back' to humans" (Taussig 1993: 97).

All the members of the chorus are black and it's the chorus that performs the most wondrous mimetic feats of the production. Disney here is appropriating black bodies in a move that evokes the alleged "primitive-ness" of Africa and the animals and humans who inhabit it.[3] It is not just any bodies, but black bodies who morph into extravagant foliage, undulating grasslands, the animals of the savannah. These "primitives," the production seems to suggest, are capable of the wonder of mimesis, a beautiful interchange between diverse forms.

In this evocation, Disney is sharing in a familiar trope whereby modernity conjures the "primitive" as the way by which it can think mimesis, recall mimesis to itself, while at the same time attempting to suppress or dominate both mimesis and the "primitive" body through whom it is perceived. Taussig, following in the footsteps of the early Marx, uses this trope differently in his imagining of a radical version of mimesis. Marx used the primitive practice of fetishism to help develop a materialist theory of a sensuous, mimetic, relationship to objects. He was looking for a certain animate quality in all things that would suggest their mutual interrelationship, relation rather than domination. William Pietz, in his own reading of the early Marx on this point, argues that Marx used the "'savage' subject of religious fetishism" (Pietz 1993: 143) as a sort of judge or measure of capitalist fetishism. Pietz writes: "The materialist subject of this radically human ground is . . . located by Marx in the maximally alien perspective of the primitive fetishist, a cultural other for whom material conditions are themselves spiritual values" (Pietz 1993: 143). For Marx, the primitive fetishist (along with the proletariat) has an outside perspective from which to identify capitalist fetishism: he can see that the apparently animate commodity does not share with the fetish its quality of radical intersubjectivity. Taussig pushes this glimpse of the primitive fetishist further in working to formulate the difference between capitalist commodity fetishism and a post-capitalist fetishism.

> Post-capitalist animism means that although the socioeconomic exploitative function of fetishism . . . will supposedly disappear with the overcoming of capitalism, fetishism as an active social force inherent in objects will remain. Indeed it must not disappear, for it is the animate quality of things in post-capitalist society . . . that ensures what the young Marx envisaged as the humanization of the world.
>
> (Taussig 1993: 99)

The stunning mimetic operations on stage at *The Lion King* may open briefly onto a glimmer of this animate quality of things, a humanization of the world. But if so, that window is just as quickly closed. The show takes its place as an instance of the more familiar tendency of modernity . . . to conjure the "primitive" and mimesis, in order to foreclose on its possibilities by surrendering it to the market. What might be thought to be the primitive fetish onstage becomes an alibi for the capitalist fetish. Each character onstage is, after all, already a Disney character, magically alive. The onstage Mufasa, that marvelous interplay between human and animal body, is a commodity fetish enacting the life of another commodity form, the child's playsuit, endlessly replicated on the shelves of the Disney store directly adjacent to the theatre lobby, just steps away from the doors into the theatre itself.[4] The child (or adult) compelled by the evocation of "primitive" mimesis on stage will be drawn back to the store, to the playsuits and toys that will help children "become like" the characters. They'll be drawn to products that are the means of becoming as life like as the character on stage.

The first glimpse of the puppets/performers is when they process from the back of the house and on to the stage. Because the doors of the store open directly into the theatre's lobby, the animals/actors parading down the aisles seem to be coming from the store. They seem to be their commodity parents translated, come to life and flowing down the aisle in what Ben Brantley described in his *New York Times* review as "the transporting magic wrought by the opening ten minutes of *The Lion King*" (Brantley 1997: E1). They link store to stage as the pathway through which human embodiment of commodities brings them to life. And the ad in the program quoted at the beginning of this chapter, "Enjoy your audience with the King. And remember, even in the jungle, American Express helps you do more," directs audience members, performers/consumers, in a reverse trajectory, American Express card at the ready, from theatre back into store, moving along the magical continuum where "things" are brought to life. And, indeed, after the intermission, the theatre was full of shopping bags stuffed with *Lion King* playsuits and toys.

The translation of the primitive into the commodity has a history in the modernist high art tradition in which Disney has situated *The Lion King*. In its choice of this director and her style, Disney made a clear decision to seek to establish the show on the terrain of high art. In hiring Taymor, an experimental theatre artist, to stage *The Lion King*, Disney bought for itself a rhetoric that attempts to distance the show from the world of the market and of the commodity and surrounds it, instead, in a discourse of "the human spirit." For instance, Taymor, seeking to differentiate her work from its highly commodified film parent, says that showing the labor of the humans animating their puppet carapaces means that she's able to achieve something "human" that special effects in films are unable to do. The puppeteers give us a chance to connect to the human spirit because we can see it at work, see that the human spirit can make a thing, a puppet, come to life. She says in the *Lion King* program:

> Audiences relish the artifice behind the theater. When we see
> a person actually manipulating an inanimate object like a

puppet and making it come alive, the duality moves us. Hidden special effects can lack humanity, but when the human spirit visibly animates an object, we experience a special, almost life-giving connection.

Certainly a critic like Linda Winer is sold on the show as high art as she melts at the revitalization of Disney's magical capitalism on the wings of this "enchanting" show. Clearly accustomed to differentiating herself from the hoi polloi and their crass consumerism, Winer sees the show as Disney rising above its own corporate greed, which is most evident in its global reproduction of itself:

> When Disney made its first assault on Broadway with *Beauty and the Beast* we were dispirited by the laziness of sprawling corporate-culture ambition. Instead of some state-of-the-art Hollywood wizardry or even ordinary modern Broadway know-how, the best we got from the legendary entertainment giant was a tracing paper blow-up of a cartoon hit – just creaky old children's theatre at Broadway prices. That show is in its fourth year now, with cash-happy clones around the planet, and Disney would seem to have no possible reason to change the formula. . . . [But] hold on to your Mickey souvenirs. Disney opened *The Lion King* . . . and both the show and the playhouse are enchanting. If this is the dreaded Disneyfication, well, come on down. Disney has taken a huge risk and dug far into the theater's parallel universe to hire the unlikely Julie Taymor, visionary director-designer of rarified folk-tale extravaganzas. If this is Disney's idea of a theme park, however, we are delighted to report that the theme is quality.
>
> (Winer 1997: B3)

In addition to hiring Taymor, Disney gives the show the feeling of being "art," or an original, through the theatre architecture, which mirrors architectural features of the store. Echoing the lavish proscenium around the stage picture at the New Amsterdam Theatre, the original, auratic image in the store – the dead Walt appearing on the video screen as I've already described – is set in an ornate, gilt frame like that which might surround a valuable, one-of-a-kind oil painting.

This original is encased by a room that's an inner sanctum for the reverent display of artist-made originals, or limited editions, of the mass reproduced objects in the larger store. It's as if the performer/consumer were directed into a kind of pilgrimage to rub up against the source of the magic. The theatre, into which the doors of the store opens, is also an inner sanctum, where the performer/consumer can gain access to the source of the magic: a real, living, breathing form of the commodity, one that cannot be, *exactly*, reproduced. The objects on stage, those carapaces, are a translated form of the commodity, Simba or Nala, that, unlike the costumes at the theme parks, only an artist like Taymor could make or envision.

By framing the show as high art, Disney attempts to make *The Lion King* into the original that it never was. It's an attempt to make it a unique, one of a kind, object-with-aura, that seemingly belies its long-standing circulation in the form of the film, the video, and the spin-offs into playsuits and toys. This construction of the show as the kind of original that constitutes high art is an operation that facilitates two processes. It makes it possible to conjure the "primitiveness" of the African body and its mimetic powers while simultaneously dominating the primitive by moving it into circulation on the market as a commodity. Hal Foster's (1985) analysis of the modernist appropriation of African art in the Picasso exhibition at New York's Museum of Modern Art can illuminate the commodification of mimetic allure, pointing out that the very positioning of mimesis within a high art frame gives it exchange value, or commodifies it. He says:

> The tribal object with its ritual/symbolic exchange value was put on display, reinscribed in terms of exhibition/sign exchange value. In this way, the potential disruption posed by the tribal work – that art might reclaim a ritual function, that it might retain an ambivalence of the sacred object or gift and not be reduced to the equivalence of the commodity – was blocked. And the African fetish, which represents a different social exchange, became another kind of fetish: the "magical" commodity.
>
> (Foster 1985: 193)

As in the Picasso exhibit, in Taymor's production the African trope is summoned in order to evoke the original allure of the primitive fetish – its suggestion of the "palpable, sensuous connection between the very body of the perceiver and the perceived" (Taussig 1993: 21). By presenting the musical in a high art key, the primitive and its mimetic qualities appear to be in some rarified space above the market, where critics like Winer like to imagine them. But, as Foster says about the Picasso exhibit, so too the display of the primitive fetish in the already highly commodified context of Disney shapes its mimetic possibilities in the interest of the corporation. Its radical transformative potential is blocked, its mimesis remaining in a safe space bounded by market exchange. It becomes Disney's "magical commodity." The African on stage at *The Lion King* is the property of the market, even more valuable there because it has the valence, or aura, of high art. The African body in this "enchanting" show becomes the magical source of magical capitalism to which, American Express card in hand, we hope to surrender ourselves.

Historical echoes

Subjectivity and the commodity: sales in the slave pens

The specifically African body has had a place before in capitalism's drive to appear humans as commodities.

Walter Johnson (1999) has written, in his book *Soul by Soul*, about the preparation of slaves for sale in the holding pens of New Orleans. The slaves held in these pens were collected by traders from all over the south. Once in the pens, they were manufactured as saleable products through techniques aimed at producing them as a copy of themselves, a made up version of the real. The slaves were turned loose from their shackles and allowed to rest and heal. They were fed a fattening diet, and made to exercise and dance to improve muscle tone. Their gray hairs were blackened with dyes, and skin that revealed ill health or exhaustion was polished up with oil or grease. They were visited by doctors for superficial medical care. And the traders provided them with clothes; costumes that were carefully chosen to give them a look of cleanliness and decency.[5] The men, though, were usually costumed identically. This, the traders hoped, would eliminate the details of each individual so that disqualifying idiosyncrasies would be less likely to occur to the buyers.

Because the slaves had been disassociated from any of their history (unlike slaves who were sold from a specific plantation or owner), there was little verifiable evidence of their condition, their capabilities, or their temperament. As a result, the traders categorized them according to an established set of criteria, which yoked the slaves together as abstract categories of displayed merchandise. They were grouped according to their relative "prime," as in Prime No. 1, 2, 3, etc. They were also divided into racial categories according to skin color: Negro, Mulatto, Quadroon, etc. Then the buyers arranged them for inspection according to height, with women on one side of the display room and men on the other.

But once these abstract qualities intended to facilitate market exchange had been assigned, buyers added to them with sales pitches designed to re-present the slaves as "people," each with his or her unique history. The slaves were also directed in performances of this made up self, (in their commodity form), that would be watched by buyers: they might be instructed in dancing, acting happy while playing cards, or talking in a certain way about their "history." Here's Johnson's description of what happened in the slave pens:

> The traders had to make a pitch. In the slave pens, the traders pitched their slaves by telling stories that seemed to individualize and even humanize the depersonalized slaves. They breathed the life of the market into the bodies, histories, and identities of the people they were trying to sell, by using a simulacrum of human singularity to do the work of product differentiation.
>
> (Johnson 1999: 124)

The slave, to be successful as a commodity, had to acquire the properties of the human of which he or she was a copy. The slave, evacuated of humanity, had to perform the commodity as a human character with differentiated selfhood. As a copy, made fungible, he or she had to enact the power of the thing he or she once was. This is sympathetic magic instrumentalized by capital. This, I would suggest, is the very kernel of our contemporary situation vis à vis our own relation to the market.

Eisner (the ogre) and the battle for the magic of the Magic Kingdom

I originally wrote about Disney starting about 1996, and on into 1997, with the opening of *The Lion King*. This period was a certain height of Disney hubris: the beautiful restoration of the New Amsterdam Theatre and the flagship store attached to it was part of a package deal between Eisner, Mayor Giuliani and the Times Square Development Corporation. The store and the show were a centerpiece of a newly "revitalized" and sanitized Times Square, a magnet for tourists wishing to experience the centerpiece of global capitalism.

But in the last few years Disney has turned away from the "magical" illuviation of the commodity into the body, and the body into the commodity, preferring instead the colder outlines of the hard sell. This shift has created a crisis within the corporation, a face-off with chief executive officer (CEO) Michael Eisner-bred raw corporatism that reveals just how important to the market is "magical" embodiment, the weaving through of commodity and human.

During the winter of 2004, the company was brought into severe crisis by a takeover bid by the communications giant, Comcast. The takeover was averted, but the tensions surrounding the bid have foregrounded the seething discontents at the heart of the corporation. Roy Disney, Walt's nephew, though only a very minor shareholder and largely inactive in the company, has recently resurged as the voice of the traditional company in opposition to Eisner, who, in the first week of March 2004, was voted out and replaced as CEO by former Senator George Mitchell.

Roy Disney has positioned himself as a purist and an anti-bureaucrat who rejects, at least for Disney, the branding that he associates with bureaucracy. He wants to establish distance between Disney and this cornerstone of contemporary capitalism. For him, "Branding is something you do to cows" (http://savedisney.com/), and making Disney a brand "degrades Disney into a 'thing' to be bureaucratically managed, rather than a 'name' to be creatively championed" ((http://savedisney.com/). Eisner, Roy says, has corrupted everything Disney stands for with his ruthless capitalism, making the company "rapacious, soulless, and always looking for a buck" (Berenson 2004: 6). Behind Roy are many Disney fans, expressing themselves on Roy's own website, SaveDisney.com, or on other Disney-related sites like Mouse-Planet. One such fan says, about Eisner and Comcaste, "It feels like they just killed the dream, magic and W" (http://www.forbes.com/). In this clash of corporate wills, Roy has no qualms about championing the company, heretofore supposedly untainted by the sordidness of branded capitalism, as a deep well of "magic;" a well at risk of being capped by a greedy CEO who doesn't recognize "magic" as the inherent source of its value.

It's fascinating that at this moment – when one corporate scandal after another adds up in the minds of Americans to a general picture of the greed inherent in capitalism – that Roy Disney rises, like a knight in shining armor, to champion magical capitalism in the face of the ruthless corporate rapaciousness of the company under Eisner. It is as if Disney is, eternally, even in the face of changing capitalism, an oasis from capitalism itself.

A pro-Roy document published on the web dramatizes the conflict in fairy tale format. In "The Emperor's New Greed," by Dave Pruiksma, Eisner, the "evil ogre," is contrasted to Walt Disney. In the story there once was a King Walt, who ruled over a "beloved and peaceful Eden, a humble kingdom." But after King Walt's death, an ogre took over and began at once with his evil plotting:

> "Just look at those fools down there," the evil ogre muttered to himself smacking his hideous lips over his great, weasel-like teeth, "Can't they see the gold mine they are sitting on? I can practically *smell* the hidden riches that King Walt has left behind as their heritage!"
>
> (http://www.pruiksma.com/)

The plot revolves around a miraculous golden goose that lays the beautiful golden eggs that somehow (there is no buying or selling in Walt's kingdom), create the "magical kingdom's" revenue. Under King Walt, these eggs, treated as objects of art, are cared for with reverence. They are what sustains the (magical) kingdom. But the ogre doesn't recognize the value of the goose, choosing at first to discard her and focus instead on other sources of revenue in the magic kingdom. King Walt's loyal faithful somehow manage to keep the belittled goose alive and nurtured, and still laying its golden eggs, eggs suffused with the aura of the one-of-a-kind, and therefore unassociated with market relations.

The discourse of the fairy tale is unremitting in the way it opposes the ogre/Eisner's selfishness, avarice, bureaucracy, looting, pillaging, and outsourcing, to the goodness and generosity and magic formerly inherent in the kingdom grown from the bounty of the golden eggs. Eventually, the eye of the ogre turns back to the goose, whose value he begins to see. He demands a frenzy of production from the goose but the desire of he and his ministers is insatiable. They want more and more of the eggs produced and with the eggs they attempt to make themselves omnipotent. Our poor fabulist cries out that "It was no longer enough just to be the leaders of King Walt's once magical kingdom" (http://www.pruiksma.com/).

This insatiable drive causes the ogre to seize the goose for himself, and take it away from its loving caretakers, the surviving retinue of dead King Walt. Predictably, under his "noxious" care, the eggs decline in size and soon become rotten. The tale has a happy ending, though, when King Walt's loyal nephew surfaces and restores the near-dead goose to health. The ogre's "tower of terror" crumbles, and all begin to "rebuild and recreate the once happy and magical little hamlet" (http://www.pruiksma.com/).

It is difficult for this author, in his account of Eisner's rise to power, to sustain the egg metaphor. While he makes the eggs the source of Disney's value, he struggles hard with trying to avoid any suggestion that they are related to capitalist modes of production (only the ogre/Eisner engages in these), even though they are produced over and over again, each the same as the last. Without the author's being able to say so, the goose is the machinery for mass production upon which Disney's profit depends. He wants us to know the power of Disney's productive machinery, the unstoppable force of the iterated egg, but to simultaneously idealize the goose and her eggs as quite an opposite thing – one of a kind, and "magical."

The awkwardness of the story reveals the uneasy positioning of the loyalist faction. What Roy and the other loyalists want is for the company to go on accumulating wealth for its shareholders through ever broadening world markets. Simultaneously though, since they believe that it is in the experience of Disney's "magic" that the guarantee of that profit lies, they have to use "magic" as an alibi for their own corporate greed, and the alibi doesn't seem to stretch quite far enough. It's almost as if, with the crisis, Disney's cover has been blown.

Eisner has, through his avowal of it, exposed the profit-driven underbelly of Disney's "magic." Uninterested in mimetic magic, and even as the value of company shares drops and revenues fail, Eisner has revealed the cheap plastic that is all the products really are, their "life" dropping from them. North American Disney stores have been sold off to a different company and children taken to the last lingering outposts find themselves confronting shelving units stacked with ordinary clothing and stuffed animals of Disney characters. Gone are the racks of costumes, the toys that invited imaginative becoming of the characters ("become a real Indian chief"). The few toys displayed among the clothes have no such encouragement printed on their packaging. At the Staten Island store, the inner sanctum has been boarded up, a shelving unit hastily moved in front of the opening. Dispirited clerks wander through the store, not even noticing, it seems, the dirty carpet, or the handprints on the counter, marks that would have been offensive to the enthusiastic cast members of just a few years ago, who took on themselves the responsibility of maintaining Disney's magic.

Roy Disney protests his faith in the "magic kingdom." But all the while he's heavily invested in the company's profits, fearing that a magical capitalism, built on mimetic desire diverted to commodity fetishism, is the only way those profits can be sustained. Eisner sees other means, perhaps, by which the Disney corporation can remain in the forefront of corporate attempts to make a final, decisive takeover of human life.

We do not tend to readily empathize with other humans. The mimetic imagination which might help us to do so is seized so that we imagine ourselves into the commodity instead. Other humans are competitors. Other people are in the way. Knowing our alienation, in some deep, painful level, we take our anger out on others. One has only to drive on the New Jersey Turnpike (or any American road) to experience this: there's a woman wearing the carapace, the body, of her Lexus SUV, bearing down on you, honking, swerving, driving a foot from your bumper. Other people are in her way, reminders that she cannot get all that she wants, as fast as she wants. As she enacts "the character" of the Lexus, the luxury vehicle, she takes on the living social force of the commodity, in the path of which the human, already evacuated, turns away, like a shade, a memory of a different human history.

This is the power of the golden egg: Being the commodity seems necessary because, after a chain of mimetic copying, and counter copying, it seems the source of life. In this way the commodity in particular, and corporate power in general, can come to seem the ineradicable source of ongoing life, whereas the human is only something in our way, dying, being blown up, suffering, needing, hungry, and decisively unmagical.

Chapter 4

Making Americans
The American Girl Doll and American Girl Place

> The values of this country are such that torture is not a part of
> our soul, our being.
> (President George W. Bush, http://washingtontimes.com)
>
> The age of global performance harbors new forms of normativity,
> new bodies and practices, new voices and discourses. We have
> only begun to scratch the surface of the stratum.
> (McKenzie 2001: 195)

In the fall of 2003 a new Manhattan brandscape opened: American
Girl Place. The store marks the astonishing success of the Pleasant
Company and its product, the American Girl Doll. Hailed by the
press as a "mix of imagination, history and values," this 18-inch,
expensive, extensively accessorized doll is wildly popular. If an
upper-class or upper-middle-class female white child was under
the age of 8 somewhere between the early 1990s and 2005,
she's likely to have had one or more of these dolls. This chapter
looks at the doll and American Girl Place as a new form of corporate performance that is integrally linked to right-wing power
in the United States. As we shall see, the American Girl products
are the means by which girls perform themselves as Americans –
a process of structuration haunted by the threat of disappearance
from the world stage upon which only the American is viable.

The American Girl Doll Company (later the Pleasant Company)
began in 1984 as the brainstorm of a woman named Pleasant
Rowland. As she recounted her story to *Fortune* magazine (17 May
2004) she was trying to buy her nieces dolls for Christmas.
She realized that there were no dolls for girls to identify with other

than those that "celebrated being a teen queen or a mommy." She hit upon an alternative; she would give girls a character from American history, a girl their own age they could identify with. She began with, as she says, "a series of books about 9-year-old girls growing up in different times in history, with a doll for each of the characters and historically accurate clothes and accessories with which girls could play out the stories." Each doll would have a "character" that the girl would "fall in love with." Rowland was so inspired, by her own account, that she wrote a whole line of stories in one weekend. She immediately began embellishing her initial vision with plans for a line of girls' clothing that would match the dolls' outfits, and an American Girl store complete with an in-store theatre where a live American Girl musical would be performed. Two years later, in 1986, the books, dolls, clothes and accessories appeared on the market. The Chicago store opened in 1998.

Rowland was already a millionaire businesswoman at the time she started the American Girl Doll Company. Her concern about the paucity of dolls for girls to identify with coincided with her practiced eye for evaluating market potential. She noticed that girls, age 7–12, had been, as she says, "largely ignored as a distinct demographic." For her they "turned out to be a multibillion dollar opportunity."

Sales to this unleashed demographic were originally accomplished only through direct mail catalogues of unprecedented allure. Then and now the catalogue features photographs of the dolls in the American Girl collection posed in richly detailed, historically accurate clothes. The first three dolls introduced were Samantha (1904), Kirsten (Swedish immigrant 1854), and Molly (1944). These were followed, beginning in 1991, by Felicity (Colonial Williamsburg 1774), Kaya (American Indian 1764), Kit (1934), Addy (slavery era African American 1864), Josefina (New Mexican 1824), and Nellie (a servant in the house next door to Samantha's – the same age, the two became friends). In the photos, the dolls are surrounded by accessories. These are beautiful and seemingly authentic miniature reproductions of historical objects. They narrate the doll's life with the help of detailed descriptions that conjure the material reality of the doll so fully that it is hard not to be drawn in, to feel one's self to be part of that life, or at least to want to be.

A description of Josefina's accessories, for instance, includes not only the material fabric of her life, her basin, towel, and candlestick, but what they are made of, ceramics, cotton, wood, linen. The descriptions seem designed to bring the little objects closer, into the tangible world of touch and contact. Some of Josefina's accessories, while still richly material, are also emotionally charged. She has a "memory box" holding a piece of her "mama's" soap, a feather from a sparrow, a bit of turquoise, a rattle from a rattlesnake, and a milagro charm, all precious keepsakes, artifacts of a unique personal history.

The doll photo and the accompanying written description are sometimes centered around a book about that particular doll. One spread, for instance, centers on Kirsten, the homesteading immigrant, who is distinguished, as her stories will illustrate, by her "strength" and "spirit." The doll appears amidst a scenography of objects that flesh out the story, "Kirsten Learns a Lesson": the bench made of a split log that she sits on at school, the ladle and water bucket she drinks from, her slate board, chalk, ruler, her "Rewards of Merit (report card)," and her "English reader," by means of which she learns her new, American language.

Without exception, parents who've encountered American Girl Dolls and their accessories rave about the quality, the integrity, and the allure these products have. This is true even of those inclined to be critically askance at the proliferation of branded products. It is also true despite the cost of the dolls. At $98 each, and along with the inevitable purchase of accessories, a typical single purchase can run to 200 dollars. By 1990, the brand was worth $77 million. Over the course of the next five years this grew to $300 million as mothers and grandmothers poured money into the company; into the dolls, into an *American Girl Magazine* and into a "line of advice books about friendship and social interactions" (http:www.fortune) that Rowland created to supplement the dolls and their "values" and "character."

With the opening of the Chicago store, her vision was complete. She saw the store as an "American Girl mecca, an extremely special environment with a store, a theater, a museum, and a restaurant" (http:www.fortune). The store grossed $40 million a year from the day it opened. Then, having completed her vision, Rowland sold the company in the same year to Mattell for $700 million.

Something new: a recouping of the human, Colonial Williamsburg, and the Bush administration

American Girl Place, this "mecca" for American Girls, is a new move in entertainment retail. In each of the brandscapes studied in the preceding chapters, subjectivity is structured and valued as an aspect of the commodity or brand, fluid, remixed, on the move. But American Girl Place, and all the supporting American Girl products, is organized around bringing into being girls who are singular, unique *humans*, with definitive character traits for which they are indebted to American history. The girls are not playing the as if, that pleasurable dissolution into provisional, commodified, and commensurate identities, as they might have in the Disney stores of the 1990s, or when enlivening the character of Tweety Bird. On the contrary, Josefina, or Kaya or Kirsten, are narrated as real girls, each of whom is equipped with a singular, defining set of values, real values forged as a result of specifically American historical situations. These historically rooted values come into being again in the form of the contemporary girl.

The striking difference in how the American Girl brand works the relation between person and commodity begs the question of why the human, defined here as that which is singular, unique, and hence different from the commodity, is being resurrected at this moment? Why, at this cutting edge store, might the production of a person shaped by a stable, coherent set of inner values take precedence over the provisional self playing the "as if" of the commodity? Who and what is this innovation of Pleasant Rowland's serving? How might it be linked to contemporary political force fields?

Beginning to answer these questions requires a look at another of Rowland's inspirations for inventing the American Girl Doll. As she was worrying the problem of finding her nieces a suitable doll for Christmas, Rowland happened to visit Colonial Williamsburg, a recreated version of the original village in which the colonial world is "brought to life" by costumed "interpreters." Since being founded in 1928 by John D. Rockefeller, corporate money and corporate vision have been the bedrock of the museum's version of American history. Though changes were made under various cultural pressures throughout the next seventy-five or so years (slaves were introduced in 1970), it was a town which originally "commemorated the planter elite, presented as progenitors of timeless ideas and values, the cradle of Americanism that Rockefeller and the corporate elite inherited and guarded" (Wallace 1996: 14). Though the final Rockefeller, Rockefeller III, left the position of President of Williamsburg in 1973, Rockefeller money continued to pour in, and Williamsburg continued to be organized around teaching five essential American values: "opportunity, individual liberty, self-government, the integrity of the individual, and responsible leadership" (Wallace 1996: 19). Colonial Williamsburg is dedicated to bringing these values from the past into the present through the medium of living bodies; those of interpreters enacting historical characters and situations and those of visitors.

Pleasant Rowland has continual recourse, as she has generated the mythology of her company, to her own embodied epiphany during her time there. She says:

> I loved sitting in the pew where George Washington went to church and standing where Patrick Henry orated. I loved the costumes, the homes, the accessories of everyday life – all of it completely engaged me. I remember sitting on a bench in the shade, reflecting on what a poor job schools do of teaching history, and how sad it was that more kids couldn't visit this fabulous classroom of living history. Was there some way I could bring history alive for them, the way Williamsburg had for me?
>
> (http://money.cnn.com/magazines/fsb/
> fsb_archive/2002/10/01/330574/)

And then it came to her that she could realize her "classroom of living history" through that new kind of doll which she hungered for. She says, "In essence, I would create a miniature version of the Colonial Williamsburg experience."

The introduction in 1991 of Felicity, whose story unfolds in Colonial Williamsburg, was the occasion for the first explicit formulation of the American Girl as something that is enacted and staged. A video, *Felicity's Elegant Tea Party: Colonial Williamsburg*, documents a live stage event/tea held at Colonial Williamsburg and attended by thousands of girls.

Upon arrival and registration each girl was given a box of party favors, including a sampler to embroider and "round-eared caps" like Felicity's. The fictional narrator, who supposedly attended this event twenty-five years ago and has now returned with her own daughter, remarks that, like these girls, she too had worn "that cap all weekend long, pretending I was Felicity." At the actual tea the next day, the girls were almost all dressed in some kind of colonial garb ("handmade by their mothers at home") or in Felicity's outfit. Without exception, they were indeed wearing Felicity's cap.

The tea began with a dialogue with one of the authors of the books, and a speech by Pleasant Rowland herself. Then came the main part of the event – a series of staged vignettes from Felicity's life. In this play, called "Felicity Learns a Lesson," Felicity learns important lessons about independence, both her own and her country's. Much of the storyline is devoted to her instruction in proper etiquette, especially how to take tea, under the tutelage of Miss Manderly. The event ends with a tea for all the little girls in the audience. Having watched Felicity, they are now to emulate the correct tea deportment they saw onstage, drinking from identical tea cups and saucers. Miss Manderly steps down from the stage, in character. She moves among the girls, giving them gentle, corrective tips.

This event seems to have become a permanent part of Williamsburg's interpretive offerings as there is, more recently, "Felicity in Williamsburg: An American Girls Museum Program" (http://www.americanparknetwork.com). This is a vacation package offering a visit to a house like "the Merrimans'" (Felicity's), lessons with Miss Manderly on rules of courtesy, stitchery, dancing, and the proper way to partake of tea, and a Colonial Williamsburg Patriot's Pass. Publicity materials warn that Felicity herself will not be present so that girls can themselves "pretend to be her" (http://www.americanparknetwork.com).

In its costumed reenactments of the historical grist and mill of American values, Colonial Williamsburg is conceived, explicitly and implicitly, as a stage on which a certain kind of American can become visible, on which people, even children, have the chance to make appearances as the kind of American whom Williamsburg frames as foundational. But there is another venue in which *showing* the American, as a person endowed uniquely by her national history with estimable character, seems central. I refer here to the political strategy of the Bush administration, that figurehead for the relentlessly growing right wing political infrastructure that will be the bedrock of global corporate power.

Since 11 September 2001, the Bush administration has relentlessly invoked the love for freedom, courage, compassion, optimism, and soul that Americans can bring before the rest of the world in a show of what they possess. For instance, referring to 9/11, Bush says:

> Through this tragedy, we are renewing and reclaiming our strong American values. Both Laura and I were touched by a recent newspaper article that quoted a little four-year-old girl, who asked a telling and innocent question. Wondering how terrorists could hate a whole nation of people they don't even know, she asked, "Why don't we just tell them our names?" Well, we can't tell them all our names – but together we can show them our values.
>
> (http://www.whitehouse.gov/news/releases/
> 2001/11/20011108-13.html)

By showing the world the values of which they are made and by which they allegedly operate, Americans are enjoined to stage themselves in ways that deflect attention from the agendas of an American political apparatus that operates according to values that seem the antonyms of those that allegedly sustain the nation. For instance, in the face of ongoing disclosures about torture and violation of human rights by American soldiers and directed by American military leadership, the political leadership ever more adamantly deploy its representational and discursive machinery to bring forth the American whose "being" and "soul" would never allow her to do those kinds of things. Americans, in this telling, are kind, generous, and truthful.

As we shall move on to examine in more detail, the five foundational American values which Williamsburg teaches, reiterated in this political discourse, are built into the characters of the American Girl Dolls, the narratives that support them, and the ways that human girls come to show their character. These values, marked as always, identifiably American, are manifested through the actions of each individual doll character in different, unique ways. Each is irreplaceable, unexchangeable – that is, human, in an equation where being human equals being an American.

The tripartite echo between the American Girl brand, Williamsburg, and the right-wing political apparatus comes from their common invocation into embodiment of an American person who is such by virtue of having certain values and character traits. This embodiment can be characterized as performance, but in a different, or additional sense than has been used thus far in this book. Though the Pleasant Company employs mimesis, with its copy/contact sympathetic magic, with its embodied plasticity of form, it moves into a more extensive, emergent landscape of performance where one's performance, and how one performs, become, as Jon McKenzie says, the "conditions for saying and seeing [and being] anything at all" (McKenzie 2001: 176). McKenzie's concept of performance is particularly useful for seeing how it is that three different social formations are mutually productive in a process by which young girls who like the American Girl Doll are used to bring a particular modality of the human into being. Deeply reactionary, the Pleasant Company reaps the benefits of Disney's magical capitalism, and moves on, unleashing through complex and sophisticated processes of imagination and embodiment a hypernationalist, coercive ethos of behavior and allegiances.

Performance

American Girl Place and the Pleasant Company product lines and advertising are striking in the extent of their allusion to performance. The fall 2003 American Girl catalogue trumpets the "power of performance." Performance is the medium, the catalogue advertising says, through which girls will discover their "unique" talents. It will also be the moment in which those talents "shine" or, in other words, when the girl can become visible in all her uniqueness. Along with the doll, the rock and roll instruments, the identical performing outfits for doll and girl, girls can purchase a "mini-mag" full of tips about how to be an effective performer, including how to beat stage fright.[1] The summer 2005 catalogue advertisement for the contemporary American Girl, Marisol, reads, "Who will the Spotlight Shine on Today?" In the advertisement in the same catalogue for the historical girls, the heading reads, "Every Story Has a Star. Every Girl Has a Story." The message is that the act of being seen by others is the act through which one will become, or be seen to be, one-of-a-kind. There is implicit in this language another message also: that there is a correct way to perform – in particular outfits and accessories

– and that girls will want to do everything they can to stay on stage. They'll want to get over their stage fright and learn to be the best performer they can be.

In his book *Perform or Else*, McKenzie has elaborated a "general theory of performance" (McKenzie 2001: 19) that helps to make the workings of the Pleasant Company intelligible. By the same token, the Pleasant Company then becomes a site at which further critical study of the unfolding of performance in McKenzie's sense becomes possible. McKenzie defines performance in its most general sense as "an onto-historical formation of knowledge and power" (McKenzie 2001: 18) "that emerges in the United States after the Second World War" (McKenzie 2001: 19) and "will be to the 20th and 21st centuries what discipline was to the 18th and 19th" (McKenzie 2001: 18). He is referring here to what Foucault (1979: 215) meant by discipline: the objectification of the subject, made legible, watched and managed through a panoptic apparatus of power. Performance, McKenzie says, operates quite differently. There is no panopticon, no centralized apparatus that disciplines bodies into conformity with social norms. Rather, each of us begins to look to the performances of technologies and organizations as the measure of their value, and each of us agrees to the expectation that we ourselves perform and that we devote ourselves to the highest standards of performance we can attain. We work to get our performances right, and, in this labor, we position ourselves as active constituent points in the coordinates of power, helping to define and clarify its potential reach. We are our own monitors, striving to reach our performance potential. Students in primary school are tracked based on their "performance" on standardized tests, stock portfolios of corporations are assessed on the basis of their "performance," microwave ovens are sold on the basis of their "performance." McKenzie argues that "perform!" is the primary injunction of the global capitalist system.[2]

Types of performances are grouped into paradigms that are constituent parts of the performance stratum. McKenzie (2001) calls these research paradigms, since they are organized by the research conducted into performance within any one paradigm. The performance research paradigms are involved in the continual testing of the most effective performances through which technologies, people, and organizations can be active co-producers of the global capitalist system. As such they are an invaluable component of this system, which is anything but fixed. It depends, as

Hard and Negri say, on a "deterritorialization of the previous structures of exploitation and control" (Hardt and Negri 2000: 52), and is configured as "a dynamic and flexible systemic structure that is articulated horizontally" (Hardt and Negri 2000: 13). Rather than power enforced from a central, or top down, position, power in global capitalism depends on its ability to spread laterally, across geographical boundaries, through virtual space, and in the bodies and affective responses of human beings. Flux is all. Because of this, within the performance stratum, and in its constituent research paradigms, what is valued is process over product, "structuration over structure" (McKenzie 2001: 132).

The advertisement and product implementation by the Pleasant Company is a study case for how performance functions both as a mode of coming into being (structuration) and simultaneously as a destabilization of that very process; the fact that the performance is always being researched means that the result of the performance, the achievement of its desired end, is always questioned, always deferred. The performer is never released from the imperative to perform, or from the act of performing – the ongoing process of structuration that is always sensitive to new criteria that emerge from changes in the global situation of capital flow and the discourses necessary to sustain its imperial drive.

American Girl: the problem of knowing when you are one

Let's turn now to the American Girl catalogue for a look at how the imperative to perform, with its attendant anxieties and risks, is insinuated into a girl's relationship to the product lines. It's important to have a sense at the outset of our discussion that there are several categories of the American Girl. The slippages among these categories are the basis for the processes of structuration and its destabilization that the company produces. There are:

1   the original American Girls, who are the fictional characters whose stories are narrated through the American Girl books
2   the oil painted representations of those Girls, in their 9-year-old form, which appear in the books, catalogues and various product packaging
3   the dolls, who are the American Girls materialized in a plastic, somewhat infantilized form

4   the human girls who are photographed in the catalogue and
     in the American Girl magazine, as well as the human girls
     acting American Girls on stage in *The American Girl Revue*
5   the human girls who are shopping for or acquiring American
     Girl products.

The fundamental slippage of categories is between an ordinary
human girl consumer and an American Girl Doll and is built into
the marketing of the doll. In Pleasant Rowland's narration of the
origin of her product, she makes a point of the moment when it
hit her that she would market the dolls through direct mail
only. She would keep them out of stores, and especially stores like
Toys "Я" Us. Her dolls, she said, had a message. She didn't want
them made equivalent to all the other tacky commodities trying
to snag the attention of young consumers by their loud packaging.
Instead, she says, "the marketing had to have some magic in it
. . . [American Girl] had to be delivered in a softer voice" (http:
www.fortune). To this end she developed a signature feature of
American Girl marketing: the primary, or even only, access girls
have to the dolls is through catalogues and these catalogues have,
as one of their most striking features, the way that the dolls look
directly into the eyes of the onlooker.

A passage from Walter Benjamin is instructive here. He theo-
rizes that aura (the original, unique quality of a thing) is present
when a thing that is being looked at is invested with the quality
of looking back.

> Experience of the aura thus rests on the transposition of a
> response common in human relationships to the relationship
> between the inanimate or natural object and man. The person
> we look at, or who feels he is being looked at, looks at us in
> turn. To perceive the aura of an object we look at means to
> invest it with the ability to look at us in return.
>
> (Benjamin 1968: 188)

When we see the object looking at us, two things happen. *It*
becomes auratic, one of a kind, and *we* become perceptible. We
become visible, as ourselves singular or auratic, through the gaze
of the object to which we've given aura.

    In the catalogues, Rowland creates the conditions for a mutual
gaze; the doll looking out from the pages of the catalogue becomes

perceptible through the gaze of the girl looking in, and the girl becomes perceptible through the medium of the doll's. In keeping the products' appearances so narrowly controlled, and in arranging the gaze as she does, Rowland takes a significant step toward making girl and doll an answering image of a singular, unique, one-of-a-kind being. Part of the research into performance that's in process here is to see how the commodity can be dissolved through calling into it qualities that it cannot, ontologically, be said to possess: the auratic, incommensurate uniqueness of a human being.

That girl and doll are meant to be answering images of one another's singularity is clear in the catalogue text. Girl and doll are alike, the text asserts, in terms of the general quality of being unique ("Just like you, each of the American Girl dolls is unique"). They also share more specific ways of being unique. Girls are asked for instance whether, like Kaya, they are "adventurous," or, like Molly, "imaginative." Josefina is "hopeful." Kirsten is "strong." Addy is "courageous." Through the intercourse of their mutual gaze, and through the suggestions of the text that surrounds these products, the girl sees herself as the doll sees her, as an answering image of the doll's unique qualities. She is brought into visibility as just like the doll, an American Girl.

And yet, even as this invitation to identification is proffered, the doll is actually functioning more as what I will call a placeholder. The girl never actually achieves the identity of the doll, never is allowed to become the doll, the American Girl, because the doll functions to hold open a space of becoming that is never finished. This becomes clear as we begin to look across the slips between the other categories I've named. Neither the doll, nor indeed any of the American Girl categories, is ever allowed, in the marketing materials, to be an end in herself, a finished entity. Who she is always seems to slip onto another category. The doll's function, then, is to invite the girl to try to be like her, an American Girl, and in doing so the doll is holding open that space of the American Girl as a space of performance. The point of arrival though, the point where one might actually *be* an American Girl, always recedes. In this performance, as in all performance, the being before you is never precisely there, in an altogether finished sense. The promise of *being* is proffered, alongside the knowledge that the performer's being is never absolutely identical to that which she enacts. Neither girl nor doll can ever quite *be* an American

Girl, but can only continually reach, through performance, toward becoming one. American Girl is less a fixed identity than a condition of continually striving to attain the attributes of the American Girl, a process of structuration.

The chain of placeholding in the American Girl product line begins with the original, "real," "historical" girls who are the foundation of the product – the girls in the stories. That the American Girls are fictional creations is made oddly ambiguous as each book about one of the American Girls ends with a "Peek Into the Past" section. This is a brief overview of the actual economic and social conditions that each fictional girl supposedly lived in and the girl is integrated, by name, into this real historical account. Here is one example: "The railroad, that 'iron horse' that carried Kirsten and her family to the edge of the frontier, was linking cities and farms across the country" (Shaw 1988: 61). Period drawings, photographs, and advertisements that carry an image of a girl are subtitled as if the girl in the image were Kirsten. For instance, in an old photo a poor girl sits on a wooden porch step while her mother washes in a wooden tub. The photo is labeled: "Even when Kirsten grew up, women's work on farms was hard" (Shaw 1988: 63). Kirsten makes an appearance here as a real, historical girl. Although they are fictions, the American Girls are used to generate and hold open an original space of the allegedly real, the origin space of the character and values of the American Girl. Their fictional narratives are merged with and embedded into real historical conditions; within the origin space, each has struggled to bring herself forth as her own best possible self by confronting the challenges unique to the American historical experience. That these girls are fictions, however, guarantees that the process of becoming an American Girl will not be finished. The fiction can never quite become the real. Nevertheless, the fictional American Girls are placeholders, holding open this historical space through which the promise of becoming, with enough effort, a real American Girl shimmers.

At the same time, though, the fictional American Girls slip from their illustrated and narrated form into the body of the American Girl Doll. The doll, according to Rowland, is intended to "bring the stories to life." Now the doll also becomes a placeholder – a space where the American Girl is brought further into material, present form. The doll opens the space for the human girl to begin to labor to become an American Girl. The girl can work to be like the doll, who is, in turn, holding open the place of the fictional/ real American Girl.

It seems, though, that with the slip from the fictional character into the body of the doll a foundational uncertainty about the ontological nature of an American Girl is introduced. What exactly is an American Girl? Is it the doll, or is it the fictional character on which the doll is based? Who is the truer American Girl? These questions become the anxious underpinning of the relation between the American Girl dolls and human girls. A strange differentiation in the use of the upper case "G" in the catalogue marks the slips between categories. It differentiates between the dolls, the human girls performing as American Girls in the catalogue (the models), and the human girls who just look at the catalogue. The "real," "historical" girls and the dolls are always assigned the upper case "G." Each of these is always an American Girl. In its address to the human readers of the catalogue, however, the upper case "G" shifts to a lower. Throughout the catalogue questions like, "What makes an American Girl?" accompany representations of the American Girls. The "G" marks the difference between the girls reading the catalogue and the Girls who they are called upon to imagine themselves becoming. The "G" is the placeholder, signifying the location they are invited to attempt to achieve through laboring to become (performing) those things that "make" an American Girl.

The young human girl reading the catalogue will also encounter many real human girls (also positioned to look straight into the reader's eyes) who, by virtue of their photographed activities, might be thought of as American Girls. They are always dressed in the same clothes as the doll with which they are photographed and engaged in activities with that doll from the narrative of the doll's life. They also use human size versions of the doll accessories. (Both their human size clothes and accessories are available for sale, and ordinary girls often make appearances in the clothes and with the accessories, especially at American Girl Place.)

But, strangely, these human girls are also referred to only with the lower case "g." Even though they appear identical to the Girls they hold, and even though they've made it into the catalogue as models, they don't seem to yet have made it to American Girl. They are marked by the lower case "g" as not yet there. Although she is performing in the place opened by the doll, who, in this chain of deferment, is also performing in the space opened by the original, authentic American Girl, even the model is not yet an American Girl. What does it take, a girl has to wonder, looking at these placeholders, to get an upper case "G?" The super positive message about girls' characters acquires, consequently, a subtler, more anxious undertone. Girls must think to themselves, "I am like American Girls, but I'm not quite one yet. What more do I need to do, or know, or act like, to get to be one?"

Girls, then, are very subtly corralled into an anxious and almost compulsive relationship to the America Girl, driven by an uncertainty about how a girl becomes a Girl. In the summer 2004 catalogue there is a page of photographs of all the American Girl Dolls, who are dressed in their summer clothing, with their summer accessories. Accompanying text, though, slips into the small "g," reading: "Just like you, American girls long ago loved summer." The girl reading the text, addressed by the small "g," is different from the Dolls shown on the page who love summer. The construction of the sentence also distances the contemporary human girl from the American Girl. The catalogue could read, "Long ago, all American girls like you loved summer," instead of "Just like you, American girls long ago loved summer." The alternative phrase would establish the girl reading the catalogue as already formed as an American. But instead, the catalogue language merely says that you are *like* American girls in this one sense of sharing a fondness for summer. Being an American Girl is, so far, deferred. You are just a girl, not yet an American one, or one with a capital G. The girl has to do the work of guessing the criteria by which she might be judged as having achieved actually being an American Girl. Does one need to love summer to become an American Girl? What if a girl doesn't love summer at all? Is she out of the running? Who gets to be seen as an American Girl, and on the basis of what?

This kind of guesswork is involved in determining how one may successfully perform within any research paradigm. We'll look a little more closely now at how McKenzie (2001) proposes performance as a continuously destabilized structuration that becomes the condition of being able to be seen and come back round to how this works in the Pleasant Company. In the performance stratum, the terms of belonging, inclusion and social productivity depend upon one's ongoing process of performance, or the performance of the organization or technologies in which one's own performance occurs. But the opportunity to continue performing, which is how one continues to belong, is not guaranteed. To be able to continue one's performance, or to achieve the goal of one's performance (like becoming an American Girl), one has to meet certain criteria that determine whether your performance is up to code. If these criteria are not met, the performance, and the person, organization, or object doing the performing, may be, as it were, yanked from the stage. The title of McKenzie's book, and its cover design, articulate the two-pronged nature, the injunction and the threat, of the performance stratum: Perform – or else.

A cover of *Forbes* magazine forms the foundation of McKenzie's argument and it features the bust of an anxious looking man in a business suit with the hook of a cane looped around his neck, hovering just inches from his skin. In this reference to the vaudeville practice of yanking bad performers from the stage, the "actor" is performing under the threat of what happens if the performance is not satisfactory. He is not yet being yanked but the presence and positioning of the cane is reminding him that that act may be imminent. The magazine cover also evokes the way that a live actor repeats a performance over and over, always struggling to maintain its quality, or even to explore new possibilities, arising from the contingencies of the evening, which might improve it. Stage actors depend for their livelihood on their ability to perform over and over, holding in place or improving a certain standard for performance. Removal from the stage, for the performer, the one who makes herself visible on stage, is to become unseeable, to be removed from the tools by which she is rendered visible. Removed from it, she is no longer a player; if the stage is the metonymic equivalent of the world itself, perhaps an unsatisfactory performance means her very existence will become questionable.

The words on the cover of this issue of *Forbes*, splayed across the business man/performer's chest, are, "Perform   or else: Annual Report on American Industry." As the theatrical meanings of performance are evoked, the title simultaneously moves performance into the world of business. The cane, combined with the words, "or else," becomes an injunction, or a *challenge*. It's the challenge to perform effectively at the risk of being rendered invisible, or obsolete, and an injunction that the performance be successfully played according to the vested interests of "American Industry."

Thus, performance and the criteria by which it is judged are linked to the question of visibility, of being able to be seen at all.

In turn, this visibility is a condition of *being*. One of McKenzie's key phrases is "challenging forth" which, in my reading, is a complicated engagement with the idea that performance as "a mode of power" (McKenzie 2001: 164) is a process of bringing into being, or *revealing*, subjects, that simultaneously shapes being seen as a structure of power that materializes corporate interests. McKenzie writes that performance and performatives are "the onto-historical conditions for saying and seeing anything at all" (McKenzie 2001: 176). McKenzie uses the phrase "onto-historical," combining ontology, or the philosophy of being, with history, to imply that the performance stratum demands a shift in our experience of being. Through performance, as a formation of power and knowledge, an altogether different historical apprehension of the experience of what it is to be will emerge. The experience of being itself, for all of us, will be dependent upon having been challenged forth through performance. These performances are situated within specific contexts, many if not most of them, corporate. Being will be a function of being able to be seen as an aspect of this context, as is the case with the American Girl. To be will mean to be revealed, through a performance-that-is-never-completed, that strives anxiously for viability, struggling to meet criteria that seem to always get deferred, if not altogether changed.

Girls drawn into the American Girl products through the place-holding of the dolls, and the Girls in the books and catalogues, are initiated into a struggle to perform themselves into being. They are challenged forth by the Pleasant Company to know themselves as beings through becoming visible as an American Girl. They are simultaneously uncertain about the criteria for doing so. Before they ever get to a store, not only the catalogue but also other print publications stimulate and hone the need to perform and perform correctly.

American Girl magazine, for instance, features on a bi-monthly basis a fresh-faced girl whose image is typically overlaid with the magazine's title, *American Girl*. The title seems to identify this girl as *the* exemplary American Girl. The cover suggests that this girl *made it*, this girl got the part, this girl has successfully made her appearance as, come to be, an American Girl. But the Pleasant Company is careful to underwrite this magazine cover with the unsettling knowledge that one must guess at the right criteria. The November/December issue from 2003, for instance, features girls who have won a contest in which the winners will appear on the cover of subsequent magazines as an American Girl. In the issue, each winner has her own page, which includes photographs of her, and of the "project" that she submitted to the judges, along with the reasons the judges chose her. Further, even given that they guessed at a "right" set of criteria, the magazine features a two-page spread with candid photographs of the winners being "perfected." The girls are shown getting their hair done, getting fitted, having earrings applied, and eating healthy snacks from a catered fruit tray. Even though they were chosen, they *still* were not yet American Girls. This spread serves as both a primer on how American Girls act, and as an illustration that there is always more to be done before one can finally make it to the cover.

At the Chicago store there is a photography studio where girls are groomed and coached, and then photographed *as if* they were an American Girl ready for the cover. They are then given a souvenir copy of the magazine with themselves on the front. Of course, it's not the real magazine – they haven't (at least yet) really made it as an American Girl – but they're given an opportunity at least to pretend to be one. The photography studio underscores, through enacting being the cover Girl, the tantalizing chance that a girl might really have what it takes to meet the criteria and be revealed as an American Girl.

With the opening of both stores, in Chicago and New York, the Pleasant Company has been able to further stimulate the shimmering hope of performing oneself into being as an American Girl, if you play it right.

Historical echoes

Girl bodies

The American Girl scene has its precedent in the relation-ships between performance, commerce, and retail spaces, especially as they were played out through the female body, that were set into motion at the end of the sixteenth and early seventeenth centuries. At that time, performance was positioned to articulate the value of the emerging merchant class, the commerce that it set in motion, and the power the commercial sector was gaining in the increasingly tense contest with the monarchy and its feudal values. The same guilds that in medieval, feudal culture had produced religious pageants were now producing secularized pageants called Lord Mayor's Shows. Instead of enactments of points in the progression of biblical history, these new pageants foregrounded the commercial potential of each guild. For instance, the grocer's pageant "represented the four parts of the world from which the grocer's commodities came" (Backscheider 1993: 38).

In 1609 Britain's Burse, also known as the New Exchange, opened in London. It was designed by Inigo Jones, the theatre designer who worked with Ben Jonson. Modeled on the Royal Exchange, it was an early mall, consisting of a large central courtyard surrounded by two galleries with shops selling luxury goods from all over the world. King James I and his wife, Queen Anne, were present for the opening ceremonies, which included an entertainment written by Ben Jonson called *The Entertainment for Britain's Burse*. The masque was overtly a celebration of Britain's imperialist trading, and particularly of the new, exotic merchandise flowing in through trade in the East Indies. It expertly negotiated the tension between capitalist commerce and monarchy by avowing, at the end of the piece, that at the New Exchange "all is given for love" (Archer 2000: 175), rather than, as elsewhere, for money. Jonson has a character of a shop boy address the royalty saying to them, in effect, that the world is unfolding itself to them for their consumption.

> What doe you lacke? What is't you buy? Veary fine China stuffes, of all kindes and quallityes? China Chaynes, China Braceletts, China Scarfes ... China Cabinetts, Casketts, Umbrellas, Sundyalls ... Christall globes, Waxen pictures, Estrich Egges, Birds of Paradise ... Indian Mice, Indian ratts, China dogges, and China cattes? Flowrs of silke, Mosaick fishes? Waxen fruict, and Purslane dishes? Very fine cages for Birds, Billiard Balls, Purses, Pipes, rattles, Basons, Ewers, Cups ... Beards of all ages, Vizards, Spectacles? See what you lack.
>
> (Archer 2000: 174)

The new bourgeoisie, then, appropriated both the medieval pageant and the Jacobean masque as performance forms. Through these highly visible civic events, the bourgeoisie worked at the construction of a self invested in commerce, trade and the commodity rather than in the monarch and aristocratic values.

The new commercial retail spaces like the New Exchange were quickly gendered, as women's bodies became the locus for emerging performances of consumption. Increasingly, as the century wore on, it was women who were seen as dealing in the world of commodities. Women performed the spectacle of commodity accumulation and became the same as commodities. In the New Exchange, women were becoming professionals, establishing shops and working as shop-keepers. This work, though, was perceived as theatrical, and the shop a stage. Like the newly professional actresses of the Restoration, they were seen as plying their trade through the theatrical deployment of costumed identities, suited to a variety of customers. Known as exchange women, they drew in customers by their fashionable dress and their shop door behaviors. James Grantham Turner (1995) says:

> The seamstress-saleswomen were regarded as fashion models who would stimulate consumption by flirtatious exchanges with their customers; in this commercial theatre they acquire some of the contradictory associations of the actress. In *The Man of Mode* for example, Etherege constitutes the New Exchange as a place of labile identity and female initiative.
>
> (Turner 1995: 422)

With the deterioration of sumptuary laws and the circulation of clothes, fashion itself had been emerging as currency. Theatre had a substantial role in undermining sumptuary laws and in making clothes commodities rather than the guarantee of identity. The theatre, that newly for-profit enterprise, flaunted a fashioned or fabricated self in a culture that attempted to stabilize identity and social structures through its dress codes. Clothes were highly valued possessions, and in an economy in which cash was scarce, even and especially the elite traded their clothes to pawnbrokers. The pawnbrokers, who were often also in the theatre business, as was, most notably, Philip Henslow, were the source of clothes and clothes/costumes for actors. The clothes of the elite thus often fell into the hands of actors, liveried servants just a step away from being vagrants. The actor thus fashioned himself, and appeared on stage, in an assemblage of clothing taken from various sources and in defiance of his station. Following suit, members of the audience at the public theatres began to appear in lavish assemblages of clothing that rivaled those of the actors. The license taken by actors and audience alike was the focus of angry criticism. Jones and Stallybrass comment that, "Attacks upon the acting companies combined a critique of the actors as shape-shifters with an awareness that the theaters staged and marketed new fashions in clothes through actors and audience alike" (Jones and Stallybrass 2000: 188).

It is this shape shifting, then, that by the mid seventeenth century is grafted onto the body of the female shopkeeper in her fashionable clothes, a theatrical presentation of a fabricated self. Her store, or the retail space, is the stage for this appearance of the self. In the theatre, actresses like Anne Oldfield both modeled splendid new fashions that staged them as the apotheosis of consumption, and performed in roles that sutured women to consumption. Oldfield was especially known for her modeling of the petticoat. The clothes and accessories she modeled were, in general, explicitly read as the end result of the glories of English world trade. This was especially true of the petticoat which was made of materials gathered across the globe. Through the course of her career in the theatre, she developed her special character type, the Lady of Quality, into a commodified consumer (see Peck 1997: 407). Through the bodies of consuming women, and women fashioning and performing themselves as consumers, theatre, commerce and retail spaces evolved further in their conjoined path.

Jane Gaines writes that, by the twentieth century and the early heyday of Hollywood features, the idea behind costuming was that the clothing an actress wore would fashion "the fiction of the person" (Gaines 1990: 199): it would, in essence, perform a person who had not before existed into being. Costumes were seen as hollow, a shell into which the actress steps. The actress moves according to the shape of the clothes, animating them. The animated costume, in turn, Gaines says, creates the persona of the actress. She acquires a "marketable character" (Gaines 1990: 198) and becomes, thereby, a fungible good that moves out into the marketplace.

The case with models, or mannequins, was similar. Mannequins were probably first used around 1857. But the French couturier known as Lucille, who was also hired by Florenz Ziegfeld in 1915 to do costumes for his *Follies*, used them in very new marketing strategies. Most stores were still displaying clothes draped over inanimate figures, but Lucille set the cloth into motion. He put the clothes over the bodies of living women who surfaced only in the fluid identifications with the commodities they inhabited, choosing from the underlying "person" those fragments that would best bring the commodity to life. Traditionally, in displays featuring new fashions, each gown was assigned a number. Lucille, instead, gave each gown a whole sentence that evoked a compelling emotional state. There was, for example, the gown called "Do You Love Me?" and the one called "Passion's Thrall" (Kaplan and Stowell 1994: 119). Eventually, Lucille developed elaborate pageants like the *Seven Ages of Woman* (1909), in which the dresses worn by a society woman enact her life's course. Each age is identified by the names given to the gowns featured in it, such as "The School Girl," or "The Hostess" (Kaplan and Stowell 1994: 119). The gowns have taken characteristically human traits, while the moving body of the model underneath serves merely to set into motion the gown's meanings.

Often the haute couturiers cultivated close relationships with actresses. In one case the designer Poiret gave the actress Spinelli the gift of redoing her apartment with the themes of his perfume, "Le Fruit defendu." In a subsequent photo of Spinelli she is standing, in an exquisitely posed skirt and hairstyle, with her stomach pressed against a mural on the wall of her apartment, her mouth posed to eat of what must be the "forbidden fruit" that the tree offers. Nancy Troy says, "The interior [of her apartment] became a theatrical space in which she, an actress . . . enacted the erotic emplotment of his fruit-scented perfume" (Troy 2001: 5). The actress/

model animates the plot that the commodity narrates as the conditions of its sale.

The Ziegfeld Follies went even further in using the female performer principally as a means to breath life into the commodity. Writing about what she calls the "Ziegfeld stage-as-department-store" (Mizejewski 1999: 91), Mizejewski tells us that,

> Another unique mark of the Ziegfeld mise-en-scène was the costume that represented [a] commodity . . . In some of their best-known production numbers, Ziegfeld showgirls formed lines of Cartier jewelry, posed as fashion accessories and brand name drinks . . . showgirls represented lingerie, corsets, jewels, furs . . . In the *Frolics* of 1919, they paraded as gems in the "Beautiful Jewels" number and as items in a bridal trousseau in "Laceland . . ." The Ziegfeld girl . . . was an influential early version of the exchange of self for commodity.
>
> (Mizejewski 1999: 96, 2, 97)

There have historically, then, been these and many other close connections between the fluid identities and spectacularizations of the theatre, the commercial interests of the fashion industry, and the female body, in spaces that merge performance and retail. When girls step out onto the stage that is American Girl Place, or onto the stage of the in-store theatre, wearing their American Girl fashions, they carry this gendered history with them. At the same, at this cutting edge combination of theatre and retail space, their girl bodies are positioned to model yet a new development in the ongoing history of capital and performance.

Mecca

American Girl Place in Manhattan opened in the fall of 2003, five years after the Chicago store.[3] It sits quietly, marked by understated and tasteful burgundy awnings, at the posh corner of 5th Avenue and 49th Street, just across from Rockefeller Center. The windows of the store's third floor are partly covered in striped blue and white curtains, which play off the red interior just visible inside.

Outside of these windows, American flags are flying. Their red and blue mirrors the store's interior blues and reds.

The interior of the store feels quiet and safe, almost domestic, set off from the commercialism, the rat race, of the outside world. Unlike the other environments studied in this book, the store's design feels (deceptively) simple. There are three floors, linked by escalators at the center of the store. Each floor is done in a variation of the store's color schemes to demarcate its special offerings. The store as a whole, though, is united by the shiny blond wood of all the display cases. These hold neat stacks of boxes in the deep, burgundy red tone that is the signature color of the store, a color also extended into the outside world in the large burgundy shopping bags clutched by departing girls and crowding the sidewalks outside.

Whereas many themed stores are saturated with technological production – music, sound effects, and video imagery – this store is quiet, notably sans technology. The first two times I visited, there were only women and girls in the store, with the exception of perhaps one or two husbands or grandfathers. Being in the store was an experience of being enfolded in the sound of female voices, voices speaking softly to one another, voices full of pleasure, girls exclaiming in excitement, or giggling. I was struck by the absence of whining, temper tantrums, tension, or anger. There were only these soft sounds, safe sounds, like an old-fashioned department store dressing room where women share the safety and secrets of very gendered spaces.

This atmospheric effect was clearly what Pleasant Rowland intended. It is, apparently, an evocation of some of what she felt during an experience she shared with her mother when she was a girl, "one of those vivid, 'grown-up' experiences that last a lifetime" (American Girl Café Menu) We are provided the story of this experience on the back of the menu in the store's café. Her mother took her downtown to the Chicago Symphony. For lunch, they had warm cinnamon buns in a restaurant. Along with the whole audience, they sang "Beautiful Dreamer." And then, in the safety of their warm and warmhearted experience, they walked down the street, a small white gloved hand in the white gloved hand of her mother, squeezing three times, their "secret code" for "I love you."[4]

The design of the store is not so simple as it first appears. It is a recreation of that alleged Chicago afternoon, with all the component parts of the experience brought together under one roof. The store comes complete with the theater, which features the *American Girls Revue*, at the end of which the audience rises to sing along with the actors. On the third floor there's a café and the centerpiece of the café is warm cinnamon buns.

Rowland's story on the back of the café menu seems to be addressed to mothers. At the end of the story, they are advised that even though no one wears white gloves anymore, even though the song from Rowland's childhood has disappeared, Rowland has created here the same sensory experience. She assures mothers that, from the cinnamon buns to getting to sing their heart out at the end of the show, she's provided them with the opportunity to recreate the mother–daughter love of her own childhood.

What becomes apparent, though, is that this atmospheric concoction of Rowland's is not really about mother–daughter love, or even a nostalgic olfactory dip into cinnamon buns. It's about performance as we have been outlining it: research into the making of American Girls, the structuration of being as an anxiety driven process-without-end.

It is striking that marketing theory that is contemporaneous with Rowland's development of the Pleasant Company targets, as she does, pre-teens (tweens), and specifically conceptualizes those children as in the process of being structured, still malleable, still in-the-making.

Alicia Quart (2003), who attended the Fourth Annual Advertising and Promoting to Kids Conference, quotes an "advertising sage" from the Geppetto Group, which does the advertising for Pillsbury and Lego, among others. He says that kids are so valuable as marketing targets because they "are in the process of becoming" (Quart 2003: 48). Another employee of Geppetto explained that the company is named after the Pinochio story because "[Geppetto] really saw [Pinochio] and appreciated him as a real child, bringing him easily to life" (Quart 2003: 49). Similarly, books like *The Great Tween Buying Machine: Marketing to Today's Tweens* advocate that marketers study the work of child development experts like Piaget to understand children as "works in progress" (Siegel et al. 2001: 52).

For the marketers, the way to intervene in the making of these children is through their senses. According to marketing theory the sensorial life of children is more vivid than that of adults. Indeed, the structuration effect of the American Girl performance relies, just as do the mimetic identifications studied in previous chapters, on the body and its sensory responsiveness. If anything, as we'll see in more detail later on, the Pleasant Company products and the store experience heighten to an unprecedented degree the relation between the materiality of the body's responsiveness and corporate fictions. In his book *BRANDchild: Remarkable Insights into the Minds of Today's Global Kids and Their Relationships with Brands*, Martin Lindström (2003) says:

> Building brands is all about appealing to the senses ... the more senses you harness, the stronger the brand you're likely to build in the consumer's mind. And, the younger the age, the better the hearing, the stronger the sense of smell and the more acute the vision. So tweens constitute a perfect target for sensory-enhanced messages.
>
> (Lindström 2003: 91)

The address to unformed tweens, and the targeting of the body and its sensory affinities, are marketing strategies complimented by what is called in the retail industry "emotional branding." Its guru, Marc Gobe (2001), writes:

> Welcome to the world of Emotional Branding, a dynamic cocktail of anthropology, imagination, sensory experience, and visionary approach to change ... Emotional Branding provides the means and methodology for connecting products to consumers in an emotionally profound way. It focuses on the most compelling aspect of the human character; the desire to transcend material satisfaction and experience emotional fulfillment. A brand is uniquely situated to achieve this because it can tap into the aspirational drives which underlie human motivation.
>
> (Gobe 2001: xv)

The first part of the paragraph is clearly about products and consumers and how to get the former into the hands of the latter. But in the second half there is a change in Mr. Gobe's language that begins to outline a shift in how corporate culture should seek to address consumers, including tweens.

First, Mr. Gobe glides with sure aim away from the word "consumer," and defines "humans" instead as his target audience.

Once he's clarified that we're talking about human character rather than consumers, he can shift focus away from materialism and consumption – the world of commodities and the desire for them – and onto what more deeply motivates human beings: the drive toward emotional fulfillment. We aspire, Mr. Gobe seems to be saying, to come into being as a person who is experiencing profound emotional fulfillment, over and above any relationship to the crasser world of material desire. This aspiration is the source of all our motivation. He is advising corporations to connect their brand to this aspiration, so that the desire for emotional fulfillment that motivates our actions is guided by and into the phenomenological and social worlds created by the brand. Through these worlds a human, not a consumer, can take shape – defined, not by the crassness of material desire, but by the emotional life. This human, we may presume, will also be more clearly connected to deep "values," which, like the emotional life, are bigger and better than the desire for acquisition. Emotional branding, in all its sensuousness, seems especially congruent with the Pleasant Company's research into performances not of consumers, but of Americans who are, uniquely, human.

The tactility and bodyliness of the Pleasant Company's approach can be usefully applied to extend McKenzie's (2001) theory of performance. Oddly, though *Perform or Else* is organized around such an embodied, theatrical image, McKenzie veers away from the body. There is in McKenzie a preference, commonly held during the years of the theory explosion, for the notion of the subject as a provisional instantiation of discursive formations – of the texts and enunciations (performatives) through which culture is brought into being and brings subjects into being. This subject, therefore, has no intrinsic nature, no defining attributes under or prior to those produced and continuously redefined in her through cultural and historical processes and imperatives. The preference for the subject defined as such often carries with it an explicit disavowal the "body." Those who take this position are sometimes even contemptuous toward those who would make claims on behalf of the body as a material and concrete organism with its own existential claims, prior to, or at least accompanying, discursive, iterative formations of the subject.

McKenzie says that success in the cultural performance paradigm (the paradigm which includes the embodied performance of the theatre) is measured in efficacy, and efficacy is achieved, not so much through embodiments, as through "networks of citation-ality" (McKenzie 2001: 42), with neither artists or activists want-ing "to ground performative efficacy in either an ideal or material presence" (McKenzie 2001: 43). McKenzie's use of his favored "lecture machine" (consisting of theorists of the digital, the virtual, and the discursive) to describe the way "cultural performance" is constituted within the performance stratum leaves other processes unmarked. The fact that corporations are making direct use of the body, not as a discursive iteration making its appearance as a subject, but as a material fact with its own clear, productive powers, is unnoticed. Using the American Girl product as a site for the study of the performance stratum helps to augment the theory of performance with a sense of how it is materially instanti-ated, to literally flesh it out.

Making her entrance/making the grade: performance at Mecca

American Girl Place feels like a place of performance. There is a distinct air of excitement in the store that is reminiscent of the lobby of a theatre before a gala event, where there might be star sightings. Girls arrive, go to the cloakroom to check their coats, and begin moving through the spaces in impeccably chosen and coordinated outfits, which sometimes are human size versions of American Girl Doll outfits. Their hair is curled, braided, bobby pinned and beribboned, often in replicas of hairstyles worn by the dolls. They behave for all the world as though they'd just arrived at the opera, eager to see and be seen. Their perfectly coiffed mothers, looking for the most part as though they're arriving from upper-middle-class and upper-class (white) New York suburbs in Connecticut, Long Island, White Plains, or New Jersey, escort the girls with the air of stage mothers. There is no hard sell here. Sales attendants, dressed in a tasteful and invisible black, like ushers, stand around smiling and holding dolls, as if each of them brings her own special doll to work each day. Lovely velvet settees placed outside the bathroom, the dramatic lighting, even the carpet, reinforce the atmosphere of the theatre, of a place of performance. It's as if the girls tumble out of their coats into a coming into being through performance, already made up as immaculate copies of the perfectly groomed human girls in the catalogue and magazine.

Like those girls in the catalogue, these girls also clutch dolls close to their bodies – their old doll, their doll they've brought from home. It's most striking, in a store full of new dolls, to see the girls showcasing their already owned, used dolls. In fact, all the publicity literature, as well as the americangirl.com trip planning guide, has encouraged them to bring the dolls. Because of the presence of the dolls, the store becomes something other than the store; it is itself a placeholder, a charged environment for challenging forth American Girls.

The challenging forth, though, begins at home. There is clearly preparation, rehearsal, that must happen before the girl is ready to make her appearance at the store. These girls don't present themselves haphazardly. Everything about the way each looks, the way she acts, evinces careful preparation and careful study. This rehearsal is intimately caught up in the doll that the girl already has at home. Invited to bring one (most girls own several), she makes a choice and in so doing she is declaring which Girl she has a special affinity for, or which one she wants to be seen as similar to, which one she wants to be measured by, when she makes her appearance in the store. Is she a daring girl who values freedom? (Addy.) Does she treasure tradition but is also open to change? (Josefina.) Is she generous and curious, ready to meet the challenges of a new century? (Samantha.)

The girls have also clearly learned (rehearsed), prior to their arrival in the store, how to hold the doll. There is an identical and highly specific way of doing this. Most likely, the models for this particular grip are the human girls who appear in the catalogue. The catalogue models cuddle dolls whom they are "like," almost always with the doll held, facing out, in the crook of the arm, both regarding their "audience" with a kind of brazenly open look. Learning this way of holding the dolls is to learn one of the criteria for the performance of American Girl. As girls study the catalogue it must become to them almost like the script is to an actor; the structure that they will take into themselves as the basis for the performance they will then embark on.

This strangely hard, bent arm grip on the dolls is quite unlike the "nurturing" cuddle of a doll usually suggested to girls in other doll marketing. There is something in it that is almost like a dare to the onlooker, or a challenge, to see the girl and doll as having gotten it exactly *right*. Without the doll as a measure, the girl couldn't be seen as having made it, done it right. The doll (holding open the place of American Girl) is who the girl aspires to become. The tight hold locks her audience's eye into a focused look at each corresponding detail between doll and girl, seeing if those details match up, seeing if the girl is, in fact, like the doll. The girl is dependent on this outside observer. Hers is not an internalized relationship with a doll in which she is developing her nurturing skills, and feels for herself her own satisfaction in the relationship. Nor is it about a girl satisfying her own subjective sense of what it might mean to be like the doll. This is about performance assessment. Girls study and acquire a performance assessment presentation of doll and self.

The girls in the store may not, like the girls in the catalogue, be dressed identically to the dolls they hold. After all, the criteria for being an American Girl are based on inner character traits that the girl desires to be seen as having. But at the same time there appears to be a general way of appearing as an American Girl that all American Girls can be recognized by, even as each has a unique character. There is a remarkable generic correspondence between the look and bodily comportment of the human models in the catalogue, the girls appearing in the store, and the dolls they carry. The girls reproduce in themselves the way that the models comb their hair into exacting styles, arrange their faces into pleasant, contented, and smooth visages of scrubbed perfection, and dress their bodies in clothes that, if not identical to the dolls', have a distinct American Girl style; the clothes, too, are pleasant. They sheath the girls' bodies in a way that resists the body revealing trends of contemporary pre-adolescent and adolescent mall fashion. The dolls, of course, are pre-made into accordance with these criteria. And in the girls there is the same control and discipline of gesture and of bodily stance that appears in the models. There is, finally, the same eagerness *to be seen*, in model, girl, and in the doll, who is, after all, looking out hungrily for her audience, held in the crook of the girl's arm. The performance/appearance in the store, then, seems to consist not only in trying to successfully be an American Girl defined by specific character traits, but also in having mastered the criteria for how one looks and acts in one's body as one is performing. It is the outward manifestation of inward character. A girl must be well-scrubbed, well-groomed, and well-rehearsed.

There is another performance assessment criterion linked to bringing the doll from home. By carrying the doll the girl is avowing her own place in that *chain* of American Girl placeholders stretching back to the "real," "historical" American Girls. In addition to bringing herself into a being that is characterized by the particular doll she's chosen to bring, she is establishing herself as a link to the past. As a function of taking her place in the chain, signified by the presence of the doll she carries, the girl is performing her *pedigree*. That is, she is bringing into being the American character traits and values unique to a particular Girl, but she is also situating those values (her values) in a lineage. She can prove her ancestry, her deep roots in the coming into being of America itself. Pedigreed Americans, real Americans, are those who bring the values of the American past into the present. The self-conscious insertion of the self into the chain of placeholders, the performance with the doll that entitles her to a certificate of pedigree, is another criterion for the structuration of the American Girl, for research into her becoming.

The Pleasant Company backs up this production of pedigree by its association with Colonial Williamsburg and the Heritage Movement from which it sprang, the influence of which reverberates through American Girl Place with every credit card swipe. The chain of American history moves back, doll by doll, to its founding moment in Williamsburg. That lineage is a "chronicle," according to Colin G. Campbell, director of Colonial Wiliamsburg, "of adversities overcome, of problems solved, and of applying the lessons of the past to the difficulties of the present" (http://www. history.org/foundation/). From this history the American has emerged, in Campbell's words, as "the last, best hope of earth" (http://www.history.org/foundation/). The heritage movement has been from its beginning moments invested in the construction of this American lineage as the model by which all those people living in American might be brought to conform with a highly conservative set of patriot ideals. For instance, the founding mothers of the Heritage Movement were especially concerned with how to make Americans out of immigrant children. Among their first ideas toward this end was that they should work to preserve historic sites. In 1900, Mrs. Townsend, the chairwoman of the Van Cortland House Committee in New York, said that the "Americanizing of the children, by enlisting their interest in historical sites and characters has a great significance to any thinking mind – the making of good citizens of these many foreign youth" (Wallace 1996: 8).

The visit by some 3000 young girls to Colonial Williamsburg, documented in the video that I've already described, *Felicity's Elegant Tea Party*, is a spectacular example of what the heritage women had in mind. Remember that the girls who came to tea, watching the live theatre vignettes of episodes in Felicity's Williamsburg life, and taking lessons from Miss Manderly, were, for the most part, dressed either in colonial costumes or as the new doll Felicity herself. (Many of the mothers in attendance were also dressed in colonial costumes.) In this bizarre scenario, Rowland has girls immersed in the "living history" setting of Williamsburg, somehow ensuring that most mothers and daughters would appear in costume, providing the hat to top off being like Felicity. The girls watch the onstage Felicity actress performing as the "real" Felicity character passing through her personal challenges to become, truly, an American Girl. Here, prior to either of the American Girl stores opening, Williamsburg itself is called upon as an embodied research site, the place to rehearse the calling into being of an American Girl, perhaps the most pedigreed American Girl of all, Felicity.

As it downplays its obvious investment in selling product and amassing huge amounts of profit, and foregrounds its vital role in teaching girls American values, character and history, the Pleasant Company is also echoing the Heritage Movement. The movement was initiated as early as the Civil War by a ruling, landed elite uncomfortable with the effects of an increasingly voracious capitalist market on the traditional social distinctions upon which they had depended. It was important to them to preserve the American character as that which was separate and distinct from the leveling effects of commerce, the surrendering of all things, including identity, to buying and selling.

Here is how the Pleasant Company frames itself: it doesn't trade in plastic dolls made in China (though it does) – it trades in American Girls, in a kind of evocation of history which is translated into the bodies of living girls interested more in history than in materialist acquisition. As in the Heritage Movement, and as in, not coincidentally, the discourse of the American right wing, what matters is the bringing forth of an American character that is forged by struggle and characterized by a deep human goodness from which crass consumerist interest is absent. This character will become visible to the world through the public, performing face of ordinary Americans. In one address Bush says, for instance:

> Our nation was born in that spirit [of courage and optimism], as immigrants yearning for freedom courageously risked their lives in search of greater opportunity . . . Too many have the wrong idea of Americans as shallow, materialistic consumers who care only about getting rich or getting ahead. But this isn't the America that I know. Ours is a wonderful nation, full of kind and loving people. Our college students and those who travel abroad for business or vacation can all be ambassadors of American values. Ours is a great story, and we must tell it – through our words and through our deeds.
>
> (http://www.whitehouse.gov/news/releases/
> 2001/11/20011108–13.html)

Pleasant Rowland has shaped the kinds of challenging forth that were initiated in the Heritage Movement and in Colonial Williamsburg to a retail environment where the challenge to perform becomes a networked link in a constellation. This constellation sutures the bodies of young girls to the global imperatives of the right wing and the corporate power to which it gives political agency and to a particular construction of American historical lineage. Mothers, grandmothers and girls who are buying these dolls are not paying for a plastic object. They are paying for this performance opportunity, a chance to belong in a performance driven world where the American appears before, downstage of, all others. And for this value, people will clearly pay dearly. The girls who flock to American Girl Place show a readiness to be performance driven; it's as if they've gotten insider information alerting them to the fact that to be situated on the side of power is to *perform*, and to perform right.

Checking and correcting: the hair salon

After checking their coats in the cloakroom on the second floor, girls travel through the store according to the itinerary that has, most likely, been laid out in advance. The day at American Girl Place will be structured by these reserved events. The literature on the store available on the web encourages making reservations in advance for the café and theatre, and invites girls to visit the hair salon early in their visit since it is first come, first serve.

The salon is at the back of one area of the first floor of the store, in a boutique featuring contemporary clothes for American Girl dolls, and matching clothes for human girls.[5] It features a long pink counter on which are set doll size beautician chairs. Behind the counter, lining the back wall, there's a mirror that extends onto the ceiling so that girls can see themselves, the dolls and the hair stylists behind the counter simultaneously and from multiple angles. The mirrors are lit theatrically, with dressing room lights. The idea of the salon is that girls bring their dolls to have the doll's hair either refurbished or restyled. Large pictures of possible styles to choose from line the back wall. Depending on the complexity of the style, the price range is from $10 to $25. There are about six stylists behind the counter, each an expert in techniques for caring for American Girl doll hair (unsnarling it), and in fancy hairdos. With her doll size spritzers, combs, brushes, and curling irons, the stylist goes to work on a doll, combing, twisting and tying the doll's hair into a smoothed perfection. Flanking the beautician's area there are displays of the same doll size hair grooming tools for sale.

The salon has simultaneous functions, the most clear of which is the reinforcement of constantly bringing into being the generically identifiable American Girl; the scrubbed face, the composed and pleasant expression, the impeccably assembled outfit, and, most important of all, the hair. A doll whose hair might have become tangled since it was bought can be restored to perfection or, if she arrives at the store in the perfect American Girl-ness, she can get a new style, thereby reinforcing the idea that the labor of becoming an American Girl is never over, never exactly accomplished.

Further, in the mirrored images at the salon, the girl can assess how she is doing with her performance. She can apply criteria both to the reflected image of herself with her own doll, and to the reflected images of the other girls and dolls who are present in the same field of vision. The mirrors invite the anxiety inherent in assessment. Do I look all right? Do I need to fix anything? Whether she is wearing a contemporary or historical outfit, there are standards for assessment. Do I really look like an American Girl looks? When people see me, will they see an American Girl?

The presence of the salon, and way that the Pleasant Company urges it as girls' first in-store destination, indicates that the company is concerned that when the dolls are at home, off site, away from Mecca, they've not been treated as the placeholding American Girls they are meant to be. Although one of the signature features of the American Girls is their hair, long, luxurious, ultimately shapable, stylable and remakable, this hair also tends to become impossibly snarled, impossible to keep perfected. When this happens, girls tend to lose interest in the dolls; it's as if they themselves yank the doll offstage, and consign it to a shelf to collect dust along with other forgotten toys. The doll becomes what it is – a commodity. Giving priority to the hair salon as a kind of entryway feature of the store makes sense for the Pleasant Company. Restoring the doll's hair rescues the doll from being a commodity, restoring to it its singular uniqueness as an American Girl. Once the doll is restored, it regains its function as a placeholder for the human girl's performance, as the child is lured back into the challenge of making her self seen as – like the doll – an American Girl.

Lady-like conversation: the café

A girl's mother or grandmother may have made reservations at the café for brunch, lunch, two different afternoon teas, dinner, or a birthday party. The environment, and dining in it, layers its own messages about the deportment of a uniquely American Girl, its own standards of performance assessment, onto those of the salon. Done in delicious hot pink, black and white, in patterns of stripes and florals, with white linen tablecloths, and soft classical music, the café is intended as the locus of the shared intimacy of the female experience, an oasis within the oasis of the larger store. It is a retreat for rest, nourishment and conversation but also a place for the bringing forth of little ladies.

Waiters in hot pink aprons edged with black approach the girls as if they were small adults. The waiters work with the care, deference and invisibility that they would in a high-end restaurant. The girls are clearly expected to respond in kind to the impeccable manners with which the waiters treat them. The white linen napkins are wrapped in daisy-decorated hair elastics that most girls leave the café wearing in their hair.[6] There are crystal classes, white china, and cups with saucers. All of this works as a signal that this is a place where certain standards for well mannered and sophisticated behavior are expected. As Julia Moskin (2004), writing a front page feature article on the store for the Sunday *New York Times* reports:

> Like a handful of New York's most elegant restaurants, the American Girl Café does not serve soda. The iced tea is unsweetened, and for dessert, there is, among other things, vanilla custard pierced with shards of candied lemon peel and served in a teacup made of dark chocolate . . . Embraced by banquettes, plied with smoked salmon and shortbread, and served tea from china pots, American girls here learn the ways of ladies who lunch.
>
> (Moskin 2004: 32)

The dolls are also central to this lady-in-training café experience. A centerpiece of the café are the black and white striped, doll-sized booster seats, provided so that the doll the girl is carrying can sit and eat with her. If the girl doesn't have a doll, she can borrow one from the café. Though the fancy foods described above are available, the pride and joy of the café is clearly the foods it serves that are taken from the historical lives of the American Girls, an idea which Rowland has also borrowed from Williamsburg, where visitors can eat historical food and whose website publishes recipes for those foods. Here, however, the cuisine is shaped to its juvenile audience, served up as "kid's food" without losing its "historic" flavors and its authentic American aromas.

"The American Girls Tea" begins with the "Warm Welcome," which is the American Girls Cinnamon Buns. These are followed by a four-tiered green Vaseline style glass tea tray presenting the "Savory Treats." These are foods that the American Girls ate. There are, for instance, "Josefina's corn bread muffins with chicken salad," and "Felicity's Virginia ham and cheese stars," little sandwiches cut in a star shape and decorated with an American flag. For dessert there is "Molly's Victory Garden Chocolate Mousse Flowerpot," which is served in a little translucent pot filled with chocolate mousse and sprinkled with Orio cookie crumbs to simulate earth. The pot has a white fabric daisy "growing" from it.[7] Each of these foods is an edible replica of the doll-size artifacts displayed downstairs in the "museum." As artifacts, the foods are placeholders for this real food, which becomes a form of ingestible pedigree, pedigree literally made bodily substance, a direct sensory assault on a tween, that person-in-process.

One of the central themes of the American Girl stories is how the less judicious tendencies, the less desirable emotions and actions of the girls are disciplined. The reshaping of these behaviors is one of the central ways through which their truly American characters are forged. It is how they become pleasant.[8]

As the behaviors of the girls change for the better, the diversities of their particular pasts lose definition. The tea tray becomes a centerpiece for this leveling, disciplining process as the wild variety of history is channeled into dainty bite-size foods, roped into the decorum of presentation. The white linen, the china, the watchful presence of the American Girl (doll) herself, along with the tea tray, anticipate decorous behaviors in the girls, an agreed upon understanding of the way that a girl is to bring the American pedigree into visibility. The degree of constraint suggested throughout the store, as here in the café, is remarkable.

In the café I watched a mother with a boy and a girl and a grandmother with her two granddaughters labor over a little white and black box filled with slips of paper. Each slip of paper has a different question printed on it. The questions are intended to initiate conversation. My waiter explained to me that these are called "table talkers," and I later saw that they're available for sale, complete with the little black and white box, in the souvenir area outside the café. The clear implication of the questions is that girls have pleasant conversation while eating delicate foods and that they need help in learning how to have this pleasant conversation which, at the same time, is instructional and provides a moral compass. The mother and the grandmother, eager for the performance in the café to be done correctly, smiling strained and nervous smiles (after all, they are the (stage) mother of the American girl-in-the-making), reached right into the box and leaned across the table to gently ask questions like, "Have you ever been homesick? What is a good cure?" and "Is call waiting on the telephone a good thing or a nuisance?" and "Which of your teachers will you remember forever? Why?" and "What's one word you'd use to describe yourself? Think think think before you answer."

Interestingly, the girls I watched and listened to tried to escape from the pressure of the questions, the food, and the manners expected of them. They distinctly tried to resist them, even if, for a while they tried to be "good girls" and comply. As in the case of the salon and restoring dolls' hair, it seems that the Pleasant Company is attentive to the ways in which real little girls may resist the imperative to perform; hence the multiplicity of types and genres and forms of correctives built into the girls' relation to American Girls. Each mother and grandmother tended to lean over and into her daughter or granddaughter's body, trying to suppress the aural and visual disobedience of the children and reshape it into the correct public appearance expected of all of them. Each grew increasingly frantic under the pressure of performing the correct conversation, but kept herself in check. The boy (the only one in the café) was obsessively absorbed in his Game Boy, slumped at the table, absolutely incommunicative. The mother whispered repeatedly to him, in fiercer and fiercer tones, to shut it off, but couldn't allow herself to become publicly angry and betray her own ability to comport herself correctly. I heard her whisper, "I expect you two to act like ladies and gentlemen." At the other table, one of the granddaughters exclaimed over Kit's sandwiches, "Cream cheese and cukes, gross!" Her grandmother, at the edge of patience, summoned her most genteel grace to lean over the table to *whisper* her remonstrance.

The girl's performance in the café, with the American Girl doll tucked into her own little chair, "eating" the foods she ate in "real" history from her own little set of china, is a performance during which the challenge is to try to learn how to stay on stage. The threat of having her granddaughters not live up to this challenge, to be deemed unstageworthy, is what worried that grandmother. She seemed to understand her "role" in supporting the girls' performance.

Just as in the early years of the Heritage Movement women were conceptualized as the guardians of American history and values, the Pleasant Company flatters mothers and grandmothers into seeing themselves as part of a lineage of women who have brought into being a definitive and influential American character. This is evident, for instance, in the cover blurb for a book called *The Best That I Can Be*, a book of inspirational quotes garnered from the American Girl stories and meant to accompany the contemporary girl as her own character is forged. The blurb promises that this book will help girls realize that they are "part of a long, proud line of daughters, mothers, and grandmothers

who have profoundly affected their country and their world."
Further, the quotes from the stories will help them meet their own
challenges with "strength and courage."

In the American Girl stories, older women are responsible to
a large degree for that disciplining of the Girls' wayward tendencies. Josefina's overwhelming curiosity, for instance, causes her to
break a precious jar of medicinal herbs that she had been cautioned
never to go near. The woman healer to whom the herbs belong
forgives the devastated Josefina. She teaches her that people should
always be given a second chance by taking Josefina on as her
apprentice. This lesson about kindness, second chances and
personal responsibility becomes part of Josefina, even as the undis-
ciplined childishness of wanting to see what's in the jar fades from
her character.

The mothers and grandmothers that I saw had invested a lot,
both financially and emotionally, in ensuring that an American
Girl is challenged forth out of the real, messy little female in their
care. They become aiders and abettors of the Pleasant Company
in working to ensure that the girls are situated in the performance
strata. What I witnessed in the café was mothers and grandmothers
near desperate to ensure that their girls will be onstage in the
world, and stay there – protected thereby from becoming something less then American.

The "museum"

On the second floor is the "Peek Into the Past" section of the
store, the section that Rowland envisioned as an in-store museum.
This area of the store, marked by a proscenium opening molded
out of the blond wood with the portraits of the starring American
Girls grouped at its center, is a remarkable installation. Each
American Girl has her own section of this circular layout. In each
section there is one case featuring a single scenario. So, for instance,
Samantha is dressed in her birthday outfit consisting of a taffeta
dress, white pinafore and, on her head, a "rosebud circlet" that
once belonged to her mother. She is posed next to a wicker table
laid with a lacy white cloth, a "Victorian" lemonade set, a plate
of petit fours, ice cream "bombes," nosegays, and favor holders.
In another display case, several Samanthas model clothing and
accessories that narrativize other moments in her "life." All of

these are made with an artifactual accuracy and artisanal beauty of reproduction that might be enviable even for the Smithsonian Museum of American History. The centerpiece of each area though, the feature toward which the dolls and the artifacts point, are "Peek Into the Past" windows, one for each American Girl. Each of these windows looks onto a beautifully detailed domestic interior in which an American Girl lives. Interestingly, though, there are no American Girl dolls in the rooms, and the scale of the room has shifted from doll size to the scale of real girls around the ages of 6. Surrounded as they are by the dolls, it is surprising to find that the featured interiors shift to a size clearly not intended for the dolls themselves. Rather, they seem to be spaces that the girl herself might inhabit. It is an American Girl space, clearly defined as such by the artifacts included in it, but from which the American Girl herself has been evacuated. Behind the glass of the window is the space of possibility, holding open the place where an American girl might become an American Girl. Here the placeholding function of the American Girl is built into the environment of the store. It becomes physical, utterly tangible.

I, down on my knees to look into the environments, to shrink myself to their scale, can only describe the experience as being sucked in. The sensuous physical allure of the objects in the environment produces a deeply mimetic effect. The visual translates shockingly into the need to touch, to be together with, to be in the world of these objects. Samantha's interior, for instance, is all in light pink and cream, with an upholstered window seat. Samantha's doll sits on the seat next to a girl-size china teacup, suggesting that the activity of having a cup of tea is in process. The window seat is next to a beautiful big window draped in a floral curtain held back with a gold tassel. Across from the window is a white wooden dresser on top of which are a girl-size pitcher, picture frame, and a rack where two gorgeous, embroidered, pure white linen tea towels hang.

The back wall of each of these spaces frames another, interior window, through which the (absent) girl looks out. The only place in the store where video is used, each of these windows displays a short sequence of life in a more public domain: a world of boys, work, animals, social games and activities. Each video with its costumed actors has been made on location in an outdoor environment that is a historically accurate extension of the Girl's house. There is, for instance, the lovely, grassy yard and old oak trees that Samantha's huge, white, verandah encircled house opens onto. The active, even boisterous, outer world of these spaces contrasts sharply with the stasis, the calm and quiet, of the interiors themselves. In its entirety the effect is so alluring that it cannot fail to produce in a little girl an attempt to meet the criterion for the performance of the American Girl that is laid out by this placeholder; the American Girl has a comportment whose energy is inwardly directed, content, literally, to stay inside the boundaries allocated her.

The activities each (absent) girl engages in while enwrapped in this quiet scene also introduce important criteria for the American Girl performance. Each Girl has been engaged in some quiet domestic activity, or, in the case of the summer windows (they change with the seasons), a domestic activity following some highly gendered outdoor activity. Kirsten, for instance, is making berry jam, surrounded by the wooden buckets with which she has collected the berries. Outside her window, which looks out onto the woods, a bear is just departing a bucket of berries he's overturned. Samantha, in from collecting flowers, has been putting them in a large and beautifully decorated flower press. Molly is filling a basket with Fourth of July decorations she's making as boys outside decorate their bikes with similar flags and ribbons. Addy is sewing, Kit is in from gardening, her tools by the door.

The absent girl is in the act of *doing*. The *doing* (the acting) is encouraged in the human girl as the bringing forth of the historical legacy and pedigree in her real, contemporary body. This happens not only through the mimetic allure of these spaces, but also in two other forms. All the craft activities, the hands on, tangible making of things, are available as accessories for the dolls, which duplicate exactly what is visible in the windows. But they are also available in step-by-step, detailed how-to guides for human girls. These instructions, which relate not only to the craft visible in the window but also to many other related crafts, are available in the books flanking the windows for each Girl. These are short books that narrate single episodes from her life. The instructions, and the implied injunction *to do* them, comprise another sensory methodology in the Pleasant Company's arsenal. At the end of *Kirsten's Promise*, for instance, girls can learn how to make a flower crown like Kirsten's. At the end of *Kirsten and the*

New Girl, girls can learn how to sew a "friendship pillow." At the end of *Kirsten and the Chippewa*, girls can learn how to make "bird's nest pudding."

Colonial Williamsburg is likewise heavily invested in the doing of intensely tactile, "authentic" craft activities, both on-site, and as lesson plans distributed on-line and through its education center into classrooms nationwide. Its education plans are built around specific topics from the Colonial period. Examples of such lessons are "Colonial Home Remedies," Don't Fence Me In," "The Trial of Abigail Briggs," or "A Colonial Christmas in Williamsburg." Most often the lessons include some kind of craft project, recipe, or enactment. "Don't Fence Me In," a lesson plan teaching "the privileges and responsibilities free people have regarding their land" (http://www.history.org/history/teaching/fences), has students building a fence from Thomas Jefferson's own plan. "A Colonial Christmas" has children decorating their classroom with colonial era decorations, making colonial Christmas recipes, and "assuming the role of an American soldier" (http://www.history.org/history/teaching/colxmas) to write home describing Christmas as a soldier. Teachers can prepare blank journals for the children by soaking onion skin paper in coffee, drying it, and sewing it together in to a book. Children can then role-play as colonial children and write about how they helped their parents prepare for a Twelfth Night celebration. For the trial lesson, students "depict an eighteenth century court case through role play" (http://www.history.org/history/teaching/briggs).

The Pleasant Company has taken its cue with regard to both these avenues of distribution, not only encouraging girls in private, at-home craft activities, but also in developing "educational" materials so that all kinds of emerging American Girl clubs and camps can implement these doings. Hallmark, which gained a franchise on American Girl products when the Pleasant Company was sold to Mattel, offers on-line recipes for Josefina's Bizocochitos and Kirsten's Santa Lucia Buns. A Hallmark press release says that the company feels this is important since "baking seems to be the one tradition that most people have in common – most likely because of the way it fosters family bonds. It's been that way for centuries" (http://pressroom.hallmark.com/american).

Williamsburg and the Pleasant Company, then, share this selling of a hands-on, tactile, embodied learning of pre-technological, artisanal production, rooted in long-standing traditions and skills. These objects, and our embodied recovery of the techniques for making them, are evidence of our lineage, the past we come from that binds us into a common set of values. They are threads pulled through to the present from the past so that our lineage can surface in material, embodied shape. Tactile, embodied recovery of this American lineage is an important assessment criteria in the bringing forth of American Girls. It's proof that authentic American values exist prior to the market. This, in fact, is the very reason that the market should be allowed to thrive – American kindness and goodness, strength, and courage of character underlie it. Bodies, along with the objects they make to underscore, transmit and enhance American character and values, reveal the character, which, if the America haters would only see, makes America (and the global capitalism it underwrites), a benevolent force for good against evil.

The Becoming American paradigm, George Bush and *The American Girl Revue*

We have been looking at the way that the Pleasant Company product line is a research site for how to challenge forth girls as American Girls. I've also noted some correspondences between this challenging forth, the policies of the Bush administration and the practices of the Heritage Movement especially at Colonial Williamsburg. My intention has been to lay the foundation for a claim that these three sites form a constellation that is constitutive of an emergent research paradigm that I'll call the Becoming American paradigm.

I take this phrase directly from a program at Colonial Williamsburg with that title.

"Becoming Americans" was a series of storylines "interpreted" on site from 1997 through 2001 and backed up by an impressive collection of scholarly research, available on the web, from which the scripts were derived. One of the storylines built on the theme of Becoming Americans, for example, was called "Redefining Family." Astoundingly, though the article on the web that supports this script is progressive in its lexicon, and in its inclusion of slave and Indian histories, it ends with the claim that, "The transformed white American family became a cornerstone of the American character" (http://www.history.org/Almanack).

Interpreters enacted episodes in the development of the American family that led to this concluding emphasis.

Another page from the web materials gives us a sense of what one would encounter in the interpreter's enactments of Becoming Americans at Williamsburg itself. It pairs a lithograph of a colonial family with a photograph of interpreters staged in precisely the same costumes, interior and physical configuration. Performance research at Colonial Williamsburg, surely the source for Rowland's deployment of a form of interpretation in the bodies of children, has as its goal to bring forth the historical qualities of "the American character," with living, performing bodies as their proof. The phrase "Becoming Americans" seems the ideal rubric to gather together the enacted scripts of Colonial Williamsburg, President Bush's urging Americans to show the world the values they are made of, and the injunction to perform as it is made apparent in the American Girl products and at American Girl Place.

Although the act of challenging forth, making visible, is present, as we have seen, throughout American Girl Place, it becomes most overt in *The American Girl Revue*, an hour-long musical, performed by eight girls (who look to range between the ages of 9 and 13) and three adults. Tickets are $35 and shows are typically sold out far in advance. The show is housed on the second floor of the store in a pretty little thrust theatre, seating maybe 170 people.

As I move toward the theatre, the carpet changes from the burgundy of the "museum" to a blue studded with white stars that are continued up onto the walls. The red of the display cases remains, however, so that the sum effect is to create the red, white and blue of the American flag. The flag, and the star as part of the flag, becomes graphic and grafted onto the body of the American Girl in a souvenir section of cases that line the lobby approach to the theatre. There American Girl Dolls are clothed in the final costume worn by the Girls in the revue: white overalls, with a large, iridescent star, shining with red, white and blue, adorning the bib, and the words "American Girl" embroidered onto the back. They stand amidst human-size versions of the same costume with their arms outstretched toward those approaching the entrance to the theatre, as though beckoning a "star" across the red carpet. The star takes on the doubled and simultaneous meaning of America and a star performer.

Once in the theatre, girls join an intimate grouping of spectators. It consists of both girls and dolls as most girls have brought
their doll in with them and the dolls sit, for the most part, poised
perfectly on the girls' laps, looking toward the stage. It is an eerie
sight, these perfectly groomed girls, some dressed identically with
their dolls as American Girls, pleasant faces, and coiffed heads
illuminated by the stage lights, each watcher doubled.

The musical has a two plot structure. One plot revolves around
the challenging forth of the historic American Girls. It's based on
a meeting of an American Girls Club (like those which, in fact,
now exist all across the United States).[9] Members of the club have
agreed that each girl will have a turn in saying what the group
activity at each club meeting will be. Today's activity has been
suggested by the character Becky; during the meeting, each of
the girls is to enact one of the stories from the life of her favorite
American Girl. The other girls will all help by enacting the
supporting cast in these stories. This is indeed what proceeds
in the *Revue*. After each story is enacted, the girls meet again as
members of the club, dropping their historical roles, and discuss-
ing the lessons in character and values to be learned from each
enactment.

This leads to a surprisingly sophisticated theatrical event, in
aesthetic terms. The method the directors of the production have
used is ensemble based and presentational rather than representational. The girls (the ordinary girls who belong the club) are
always present on stage, even when not "acting." Those who
are taking on a character are always showing their doubleness;
they are both girl and Girl. Girls who are not onstage often sit on
the stairs in the intimate house, among the audience, or sit just
below the platform that is the stage, elbows leaning on it, both on
and off the stage at the same time. Sometimes they punctuate the
onstage action with sound effects like clapping their hands, or with
body movement that helps to heighten the emotional content of
the scene on stage. Props and scenery are minimal, and the girls
use movement and minimally suggestive objects to enact non-
human forces like trees, storms, and so forth. Three live musicians,
visible off to stage right, accompany the performance. All in all,
the essential theatricality of the *Revue* is constantly foregrounded,
as if to emphasize that the pleasures and anxieties of performance
are at the heart of being an American Girl.

The stage the audience encounters is painted in a kind of impressionistic grass and the back wall is painted blue with exits on either side of the stage. A circle of bright red wooden chairs is pre-set on stage. On each chair is a single costume element which is readily identifiable as belonging to a particular American Girl. The little girl sitting next to me, for instance, sings out, "That's Kirsten's flower crown!" The girls skip onstage, each impossibly well-groomed, in fashionable, but very "decent" girl's outfits. They are the contemporary equivalent of the clothes children wear in Norman Rockwell paintings. They are singing *The American Girls Anthem*: "I can be brave, I can be true, I will do the best that I can do," etc. Each sits in a chair and puts on the costume piece left there. In this way the show is framed by an overtly theatrical gesture of putting on an American Girl.

Each story enacted in the *Revue* is a situational conflict for one of the Girls from which she emerges with a particular kind of American value and character. The lexicon of values used in the *Revue* is virtually indistinguishable from that of the Bush administration in its constant repetition of phrases like the following: "We are leading the world with confidence and moral clarity. Our nation is strong because of the values we try to live by: courage, compassion, reference,[10] and integrity" (http://www. georgewbush.com/News/Read.aspx?ID=2955). Each story might be an illustrative, embodied example of how these values come to be made and lived by: Kit lives during the depression. Her father is out of work, and her aunt, who has also become unemployed, arrives to live with them. Kit, who initially is downhearted and somewhat sullen about her situation in life, is angry that she'll have to share with this aunt resources the family is already lacking. But all this is overcome, as the cheerful, resourceful and very energetic aunt turns everything into an opportunity. Their household is transformed through the aunt's initiatives. Kit, singing her aunt's song about using the lemons life gives you to make lemonade, learns how to make opportunity from disadvantages, to have resilience, resourcefulness, and unflagging optimism in the face of adversity.

Samantha's story centers on the moment she stands up in a school auditorium and has the courage to speak, in the face of her mother's disapproval, about what she's learned from her servant friend, Nellie, about child labor in factories. In a suspenseful moment of dead silence after the speech, Samantha fears that she's done the worst she can do to her wealthy and powerful mother. But that moment ends in a tremendous surge of applause, including applause from her mother, who rises to her feet in a standing ovation, and Samantha learns how important it is to have the courage to hold fast to her own values.

Of course, the signature chant of the American right wing centers on the concept of freedom. It's freedom that's the distinguishing trait of being American, as when the president crows, "Ours is the cause of freedom. We've defeated freedom's enemies before, and we will defeat them again" (http://www.whitehouse.gov/news/releases/2001/11/20011108–13.htm). Manifesting the "love" of freedom is essential to the American Girl performance and the single most popular vignette in the *Revue* is organized around the theme, shamelessly deploying the history of slavery into a weepy, feel-good conjuring of freedom. It begins with Addy, the black American Girl born into slavery, and her mother. It is the middle of the night. Her mother is panicked because she's received word that they are to be sold and separated. They have to escape tonight. She and Addy quickly change into someone else's clothes so the dogs won't be able to smell them. Her mother tells Addy, in a briefly grieving moment, that Addy's baby sister has to stay behind since her crying will betray them. In other words, the brief narrative hits all the high points of common knowledge about slave flight. Here are the well-rehearsed emotional triggers which are trundled out to ensure our admiration for how much Americans are willing to sacrifice when they hold freedom so dear. Mother and daughter make their perilous journey north in about two minutes of movement, while singing inspirational songs about inner strength, and then they arrive in Philadelphia.

Once settled, Addy discovers that she is not free in Philadelphia either; she's not served, not allowed on streetcars, and so forth. When she speaks to her mother about this, her mother reassures her that she has freedom "inside," and they break into a "Freedom Song." The lyrics are about how, since Addy has her own thoughts and her own dreams inside her mind, and since she knows just who she is, she is, in fact, free. The injustices of the outside world really can't touch or harm her. The song is rousing, sung in gospel style, and the audience loves it.

What Addy's story does not, of course, include is the history of slave revolts, of slave resistance, of the untold death and suffering in slavery, or of the way that the legacy of slavery continues in the economic and social crisis lived by so many African Americans today, in contemporary race relations, and race warfare.

Addy ends up living quietly with her mother, in her own domestic space, with her own little window looking out onto the streets of Philadelphia, with a tidy little sewing business. Addy doesn't need to get rowdy, or to join up with any resistance movements within the free black community. She doesn't need to organize with others around their collective lack of freedom: she is free inside. The lesson of the story ultimately is that, with guidance from her mother, she can and should become her own leader, independent of political and social life. This independence frees her from contact with any community that might stir up in her a sense that real human freedom depends on her joining forces with them. Overcoming slavery for the American Girl is apparently a matter of individual will, determination, and a commitment to freedom as an inner property of character. It is not the exercise of social and political questioning and actions. It is a lesson strikingly similar to the goals of the Heritage Movement's Sons of the American Revolution, one member of which said that the working class "must be educated out of all these crass and crazy notions of popular rights . . . into a true understanding of American liberty as handed down by our Fathers" (Wallace 1996: 8).

The *Revue* ends in an orgy of patriotism during which the American Girls on stage, now dressed in those white overalls decorated with the iridescent star on each bib, join hands with Molly, who is dressed in a red, white and blue tap dancing outfit. They've just completed the Michelle and Becky number, in which Molly's celebration of the end of World War II is enacted. The girls onstage invite the members of the audience to rise and sing *The American Girls Anthem* with them. Almost without exception, the members of the audience rise to sing, with as much fervor as if it were the American National Anthem itself, which surely it is meant to echo. It's a song about being true to myself, to my dreams. It's about having the courage to dare, to be true, to be brave and to sing with my own voice. It's a collective moment in which we've all been drawn together into a joint embodiment of a consensus about our character and values. We're making our appearance.

It is impossible to miss how overtly the point is made that performance is the way to be an American Girl. It's also hard to miss how that very fact produces again the anxiety about who actually is an American Girl: the anxiety that permeates the

American Girl experience from catalogue to store to theatre. From the outset, the girl spectators and their dolls are strangely displaced. The stage in front of them now becomes the placeholder, the site of structuration. But they are not on it. Like the relative impossibility of being on the cover of the magazine and therefore, verifiably, having become an American Girl, here they have not (yet) made it. Both they and the dolls, watching, seem to be in a position to both assess the performance of the girls onstage performing Girls (by doing so, are those girls becoming Girls?), and to assess how they might get up there, on to that stage. The message is clear; being an American Girl really does happen on stage. On stage is where you move through all the placeholders, all the sites of structuration and you become not just a star, but an American star (at least until the next night, when you have to endeavor to do it right all over again).

After the show the girl performers come out to give autographs. Who are they signing as? The American girl who got the part because she figured out how to do the performance right? On one of my visits to the store, a long line of girls and mothers snaked through the entire second floor. The girls, it turns out, were waiting to audition for the *Revue*. There were so many girls, each hoping to be the one who gets a chance to really get on the stage. If they can get there, their performances will be the instantiations of what President Bush means when he says, "We're good. We're good-hearted people, and the boys and girls of America are showing the world just that" (http://www.whitehouse.gov/news/releases/2001/10/20011016–4.html).

Let's turn for a minute to a wildly different artistic production, Michael Moore's *Farenheit 9/11*, as a way to explore just how much confidence the members of the Bush administration, like the Pleasant Company and Colonial Williamsburg, have in performance research. The members of this tripartite coalition that I've constructed, constituents of the emerging performance research paradigm, Becoming American, are working performance as the contemporary modality by which the apparatus of imperial corporate power is secured. In their creative hands it is the apparatus by which America and Americans are made visible, staged, as singularly unique, compassionate and good humans, even as unjust and power hungry violence is perpetrated against those who will not, cannot, make themselves visible, who will not become, thereby, human. In their hands, and as the film shows, research for the Becoming American performance paradigm is pulled in and through research in other paradigms, modes of power borrowing strength, assessment criteria and strategy from one another into what McKenzie calls "the power of performance" (McKenzie 2001: 159).

The film was one of the signature anti-Bush activist efforts of the critical 2004 election. As such it is fascinating and important that, among other things, it works to reveal performance as a key organizing modality of emerging imperial power, personified in this case in the actions of Bush and the Vulcans[11] so as to reveal that they do in fact deploy performance, try it out, research it, as a way to appear America. Moore begins *Farenheit 9/11*, as the title and credits role, with out-takes, offstage clips of Wolfowitz, Chaney, Ashcroft, Rice, and Bush. They are getting made up prior to going on stage, or on camera, to make the announcement that America will commence its unilateral and pre-emptive war on Iraq. What is striking is their absolute certainty about the power of their performance: they joke and mug as the hands of the make-up artists appear and brush the last bit of powder onto their face, or the last bit of lint off their collar. Wolfowitz puts his comb in his mouth and combs his own hair, and then uses his spit to smooth a stray hair into position, smirking mischievously at the camera as he does so. The film ends with the same Vulcans taking off their microphones, letting go, undoing all the apparatus of the performance they've just completed.

During this performance, framed as such by the opening and closing of the film, Moore documents Bush playing for cameras at different times in different roles; solo performances of himself as American. We see him producing his performance as athlete, his performance as a rancher who loves nature and animals, his performance as a member of the "folk," a simple, down home guy.

But, even more than this, the film makes evident the ways in which the research by the Bush administration for the Becoming American paradigm is woven in and through other performance research paradigms, augmenting its own power. It is this tendency of paradigms to soak into, support and inform one another that gives performance its totalizing power as the condition for being. It is important to glimpse the network of these performance paradigms because it is to this network that the American Girl performance research contributes.

McKenzie (2001) focuses in his book on cultural, organizational and technological performance. Cultural performance gathers together embodied performances like theatre and film and performatives, like those through which race and gender are constructed. The criterion by which cultural performance is measured is whether or not it is efficacious in being liminal, challenging norms. Organizational performance is the control on the behaviors of management and employees to guarantee maximum profitability. Its assessment criterion is the efficiency with which an organization or corporation is run and it's measured through feedback loops. Technological performance manages the creation and deployment of technology, from kitchen appliances to bombs, and is measured by the effectiveness of the technology. Although each paradigm has its own standards for assessment, these criteria bleed into one another. Recent organizational theory, for instance, suggests that a company's performance will be more efficient the more it encourages its employees toward the creative challenging of norms. In general, the performance paradigms, and the ways that performances are measured, form a mode of power precisely because they move in and through each other and, hence, become hard to stop or resist. This is "the power of performance", that super model that "both incorporates and passes beyond" (McKenzie 2001: 159) individual paradigms.

The interconnections between the paradigms McKenzie identifies begin to emerge in *Farenheit 9/11* as Moore tracks how quickly after 9/11 the Bush administration took steps to cover up any possible evidence of the financial and personal affiliations between its members and the Bin Ladin family. These affiliations were created to ensure the high organizational performance of corporations from which a telling configuration of personalities stood to profit; rich Arabs, and in particular members of the Bin Ladin family who owned significant shares of Bush's own oil companies, Bush, Cheney, and Bush's good friend, James R. Bath. Bush's cultural performance is clearly intended to create the optimal political conditions through which the performance of the corporations in which the Bin Ladins, Cheney, Bush and Bath are invested may be optimally efficient. But each of these parties also has a stake in technological performance since high technologies, and in particular war technologies, are part of what their companies do.

The interconnections between the Becoming American, technological and organizational performance research paradigms are made especially clear at one moment in the film when Moore returns to the "backstage" imagery. Bush is composing his face during the countdown to the moment when he will appear on TV to make the announcement that America is about to invade Iraq. These images of Bush getting ready for his performance are intercut with images of high performance missiles being loaded and fired. A constellation is here present, the constituent members of which are dependent upon the performance of the others; the success of Bush's Becoming American performance affects the performance of stocks and bonds which measure the organizational performance of the companies producing technology, and the performance of the technology itself also influences the performance of stocks and bonds and Bush's Becoming American performance. Each adjusts its own performance criteria and assessment based on research in other paradigms, each continues to research its own performances, and each gathers power from its imbrication in the others. Another piece of *The American Girl Revue* shows how the American Girl performance, with its research for the Becoming American paradigm, likewise gathers power from, and contributes to the power of performance; the expanding strength of the global reach of the American right-wing elite.

The second "plot" in *The American Girl Revue* intertwines into the first plot and its bringing forth of American values a staging of center and periphery that becomes, perhaps, the most insidious challenging forth of the American Girl performance. This plot centers on two girls who are outsiders and how they become members of the club. The first becomes a star by virtue of determination and long rehearsal, and the second, who must be convinced and seduced into trusting the value of performance, finally comes into her own as a performer. The story is an inspirational tale about the determination that can get you onto the stage, and also a parable for how those on the periphery of the stage are endangered. They may not have identity or viability. They become, thereby, something less than human.

One of the outsider girls is Michelle, the younger sister of Becky. Michelle is determined to be an American Girl, but has been barred by the older girls from a place in the club. She makes a "pesky" nuisance of herself demanding, as each of the girls says who they'll be, "Who am I going to be?" She is determined to become an American Girl. She stays with the club members, watching, as they do, each of the characters as they are performed.

Her opportunity comes when, toward the end of the *Revue*, Becky bursts onto the scene with the news that her friend is still sick. She collapses on stage in a fit of disappointment. She won't be able to perform herself as the American Girl, Molly. She and her friend had rehearsed and rehearsed Molly's story, especially the tap-dancing, patriotic "Victory Dance." Now she can't get on stage. But Michelle, it turns out, in her eagerness to be a player, has watched every single rehearsal that Becky and her friend conducted, hidden in the laundry basket. As a result, she knows all the parts of the "Victory Sisters" performance and can make it possible for Becky to perform Molly. Because of her determination to get out there on the stage, no matter what it takes, Becky allows Michelle to come out of hiding (in the laundry basket). Michelle gets to stop being invisible and be an American Girl.

The other outsider is Laura, a new girl whom Becky has brought along to this meeting of the American Girls Club. Laura stands out from the rest. The other girls in the club, for instance, are unfailingly kind and polite toward one another. They smile into one another's eyes, take the hands of the other girls in theirs and swing them from side to side. They clasp their hands over their hearts in expressions of mild joy, and lay gentle, comforting hands on one another's shoulders. Laura, by contrast, is awkward and uneasy. She doesn't touch anyone. She seems rigid and stand-offish. She doesn't seem to share their character, and their values. Her face is set and sullen rather than open and pleasant. She stands to the side, her brown boy-like shirt, her beige pants, making her stand out against their very feminine pastels and whites.

The girls try to elicit from Laura who she wants to be and she answers mournfully that she doesn't "know how" (to play, to be, an American Girl). Faced with this problem outsider, the club members agree that they should show Laura how they "play American girls." This is, in fact, what initiates the sequence of American Girl enactments that follows. As music begins and the lights change, the girls coach Laura to imagine herself in another time and place in the past.

This is not enough to get Laura onstage. After a few enactments of the Girls' stories the group reconvenes as the club and they discover that Laura has disappeared. Michelle, not yet a member of the club either, comes in to say mockingly that she's spied on Laura and discovered her in a peculiar, solitary habit – bird watching. The girls who, as American g[G]irls, are unfailingly kind, chide Michelle for her ridicule. Someone goes to find Laura, who, it turns out, had gone home, convinced she wouldn't be able to be a member of the club. The girls reassure her by telling her that they had to learn how to play the Girls too. Laura, they say, can do it by reading all the books and learning about the Girls from other club members like they did. Laura is still not convinced of her credentials for belonging because what is really worrying her is that she doesn't own a doll. Her parents have split up, her mother and she have just moved here, and her mother doesn't have the money for a doll.

Evidently having a doll is in fact an important part of belonging to the club because one of the girls, Katie, volunteers to loan Laura one of hers, Kirsten. She chooses Kirsten because both Laura and Kirsten are newcomers, and solitary. Then Katie convinces the very reluctant Laura to be the one to help her enact the Kirsten story. Very gradually, the shy Laura is drawn into her onstage role as the Indian girl, Singing Bird, who Kirsten befriends in the Minnesota woods. Singing Bird is named for her beautiful bird calling. Playing Singing Bird is a perfect way for Laura to showcase her unique abilities. She becomes more and more certain of herself on stage and, by the middle of the vignette, she is Kirsten's co-star. She finds she is a natural at performing. Her tendency to slip away into the shadows, into hiding, to indulge in her solitary life and habits, is sloughed off as she learns to love the spotlight. As she appears her face loses its sullen set and its shadows and takes on the generic American Girl expression: bright eyed, open and pleasant, ready with an easy smile. The other girls love her. She's slipped from periphery to center stage; they induct her as a full member of the club.

This story could be a demonstration case, a trade show exhibit, for the way that the post-9/11 war on terrorism, and in Iraq, work the relationship between center and periphery, visibility and hiding, willingness and reluctance to perform. There are those who lurk on the periphery, on the somewhat less-than-human edges of the world stage. Those who are willing to be like Americans, to take on American values, are welcomed into the spotlight, where they become, unlike those left behind in the shadows, fully human, fully participatory.

Iraqis, like terrorists, are invisible. The high performance sighting technology of military planes and smart bombs allows the military to hit precise targets without there ever being a need to see the victim, or the resulting carnage. The media likewise do not see or say this enemy. One of the central features of news coverage of the war in Iraq has been its refusal to show the bodies of Iraqis killed or wounded as a result of American aggression, or even to make an account of their numbers.

But there is an alternative for Iraqis who don't wish to remain unseen. If they begin to conform to a set of performance criteria they will begin to appear. Like the American girls onstage singing Addy's freedom song, Iraqis can bring themselves onto the stage by Becoming Americans. First and foremost, they need to challenge themselves forth like Americans by performing their love of freedom. In one of his speeches Bush spells out the deepest desires of Iraqis; that they want to be peaceful, aspiring inheritors of the American lineage of freedom. They want to be "just like Moms and Dads in America":

> Free men and women will be peaceful men and women. Free men and women will be able to realize their deepest desires. Listen, Moms and Dads in Iraq want to be able to raise their children in a society where their children can have a bright future, just like Moms and Dads in America do.
> (http://www.usembassy.org.uk/bush299.html)

Even if these Iraqis never actually live in America or become American citizens, they can get on stage by wanting to be like Americans. If they get visible by performing their love of American values on the world stage they can escape the aggression shown those who won't agree to challenge forth American values. They have the opportunity to be visible and, therefore, viable – as long, of course, as they keep doing the right performance, as long as they keep perfecting the performance.

The terrorists, by contrast, deliberately hide. Those unwilling to step on to the stage, into the spotlight, are terrorist. They lurk in the shadows. According to Bush, "evil folk still lurk out there" (http://archives.cnn). Since 9/11 the entire apparatus of power has figured the new enemy as faceless, organized into invisible "stateless networks" (http://www.bloomberg.com). Lurking, hiding, the terrorists are like animals. They *are* animals, devoid of

human powers of reason and morality, conscience and sentiment. They are to be hunted down. In a campaign speech from
July 2004, Bush says, "You can't talk sense to them. You can't
negotiate with them. You cannot hope for the best with these
people. They're running out of places to hide . . . And that's why
their actions have grown more cruel and sadistic" (http://www.
usembassy.org.uk/bush299.html), and "Theirs is the worst kind
of cruelty, the cruelty that is fed, not weakened, by tears" (www.
albertarose.org/Remember/pentagon.htm).

The American soul, as Bush remarks in the epigraph for this
chapter, is above cruelty. In contrast to hiding, lurking terrorists,
we are inhabited and motivated by a soul, which, Bush admonishes, "they must have felt like they could diminish" (http://www.
whitehouse.gov/news/releases/2001/09/20010925–5.html).
A final Bush campaign ad before the 2004 election insinuates a
comparison of the terrorists with wolves. The advert

> shows a dense forest from above and sunlight speckled trees
> from inside. Shadows, seemingly made by [prowling] wolves,
> dart through the brush. "Weakness attracts those who are
> waiting to do America harm," says an ominous voice . . . as
> a wolf pack stirs from its resting spot.
>
> (http://www.showmenews)

American soul, like the bright, open, scrubbed faces of the girls
playing the Girls onstage in the *Revue*, seeks the light – it is not
afraid to be seen. It is above all, strong and courageous, unswerving
from responsibility, and as the American Girls show us, challenged
forth from the struggles of history. The sub-human terrorists,
on the other hand, absolve themselves from this responsibility.
Speaking of videos terrorists make of themselves, Bush cries, "They
cover their faces in videos, in the videos of their crimes" (http://
www.usembassy.org.uk/bush299.html).[12]

I return to one of the questions with which I opened the chapter.
Why, after all the years of the provisional, postmodern self, does
the Pleasant Company research performance which initiates the
return of the singular, internally coherent human being? Who and
what is this innovation by Pleasant Rowland serving? I think it is
that the human has to be returned, continuously performed into
being, tested, assessed, kept operational as the contrast to the
one who will not become visible, who won't perform according to

the criteria of Becoming American, and who can, therefore, be understood to be less than human. Many of us have recognized that the contrast between the human and the non-human justifies the ongoing and virulent aggression of American power. The Becoming American paradigm is the operation for the production of that human.

The photographs from Abu Ghraib are a particularly gruesome expression of American violence, especially since they take place on the terrain of performance itself. The first photograph released, of the man draped in a black blanket, standing hooded on a box with arms outstretched and attached to wires, documents a performance, a challenging forth of the Arab, as one who refuses to get onstage. The man, of course, didn't put the hood on himself. The soldier did. The soldier is staging Bush's claims about the sub-humans who hide their faces, lurk in holes. By contrast, the American, the soldier, smiles broadly into the camera, unafraid of being center stage. In a performance that is the dark underbelly of that of the American Girls, the American soldier is, not unlike girls hoping to be American Girls, hoping that he's getting *his* performance of being an American right. He's hoping that, as a result of his revealing or challenging forth of this less-than-human hiding under a hood, *he* will get to stay onstage.

Against the background of the certainty of the Vulcans in the power and superiority of their performances, we struggle anxiously, like the girls at American Girl Place, or like the soldiers at Abu Ghraib, to stay on stage. In their different ways Pfc. Lynndie R. England, as she smiled into the camera, and the little girl in her Samantha outfit checking her reflection in the mirror at the hair salon, are each participating in the Becoming American performance research paradigm. What happens to those who won't perform is clear. They are, decisively, and often through the loss of their life, yanked offstage. This is, perhaps, why Americans voted the Bush administration to power twice and, for the most part, have supported its military initiatives, its offensives against the poor. By supporting them, we ally ourselves with the certainty of their performances and the guarantee, written into the immensity of the performance stratum, that they'll have a long run. We know, innately, that we have to stay center stage, or we might end up like all the rest of the world's poor; interchangeable victims lacking the status of the human and the rights pertaining thereto, or worse, evil doers to be hunted down. The Vulcans perform magnificently, as do their companies and their technologies. And as long as we support them, we can participate in the power of performance they can secure and they'll make sure that, as Americans, we stay at the center of the world stage. It is a new era of global capitalism, fueled in part on the power of performance. The audience at *The American Girl Revue* rises with terrific enthusiasm at its conclusion to join in singing the *American Girl Anthem*. It may just be that they sense, on some level, that they are thereby bringing themselves into being in the only way that it is possible, in this strange and violent time, to do so at all.

Epilogue

Rosalind, tongue in cheek, begins the epilogue to *As You Like It* by recounting that in popular opinion a good play shouldn't need one. But in Rosalind's epilogue there is this: a singular, vulnerable body on an emptied stage, obstinately present in the face of fashion, who shares with you her wish that something may come of the work that she has done – love, reconciliation, generosity. Such an epilogue is an act of exposure, is it not? It lays bare our desire that what we have done has meaning, will have meaning on behalf of the human spirit.

Reflections on exposure, vulnerability, the question of how to gather together hope as a political possibility: these are common threads in the work of those seeking antidotes to the gathering and developing structures of global power. We begin to once again think of the human, not for the right-wing spirit in which the Pleasant Company revives it, but because it is so necessary to say again that we must have a claim – on love, on caring – that can become the demand for a deeply democratic and just world.

As for my work, my wish is for you, reader, to have found in it recognition, flashes where you say, "I too have seen this": a form of commonality between you, me, and other readers. I hope I have convinced some of you to look differently at stores. I hope that some of you will be able to make use of what I have written here. I hope that you may have found in these chapters points useful for gathering into common the resources with which we may try to save, perhaps not so much even ourselves, as the young. It is they, after all, at whom so much of the corporate agenda is ever more virulently targeted.

To see the world clearly it is necessary to understand that there is underway an immense new redefinition of the way that power is gathered, distributed and inflicted. President Bush (and maybe even the long-lived Vulcans) are just an instance, a glimpse into the new contours of the way that corporate power is organizing and articulating itself – their precipitous fall from popularity does not, unfortunately, signal a return to the liberal democracy of a welfare state – they stumbled, made too many mistakes is all. The logic by which they proceeded will, I fear, be merciless in perpetuating itself without them. The American right wing, upon which global corporate power depends, has fundamental arguments, and fundamental convictions that demand from each of us bodily loyalties like those I've described in this book. And the decline of American "democracy" into what Hardt and Negri (2004) identify as a state of exceptionalism and permanent war is such that if and when Democrats are voted in to power, there is unlikely to be much change.

Each of the brandscape formations described in this book ensures our quotidian encounters with global power. They ensure that it can reach into us daily, unobstrusively, through the pleasures of our mimetic aptitude for imagining and playing ourselves as other than what we are. Each of the brandscapes, different as they are, are places where we perform, appearing ourselves, challenging ourselves forth, working, playing to get it right. The brandscapes are where we fashion ourselves into mutiple selves, bringing into postmodern form that "case of faces" that Thomas Dekker described in the early seventeenth century (Agnew 1986: 57). They're places where our selves play out according to an affective range, a sensation of feeling alive, which becomes, without our necessarily knowing it, an agreement to feel life as that which the corporate world builds around us.

And yet, for all but the richest or luckiest of the world, our positions, our grip on the world, our toeholds, are precarious. There is slippage all around. That it might be us who slips is a possibility that makes us continually renew the zeal with which we shop, immerse ourselves in the brand, join the real to the really made up of the brand. The mountain of the discarded, the slipped, those who maybe never had a chance to perform in the first place, grows ever higher. Zygmunt Bauman (2004: 70) calls these people "human waste," or "wasted humans." There is, in Bauman's account, and the evidence is all around, more and more of that waste, more and more who haven't stayed on stage, or even started rehearsing.

I think of Luis Alberto Urrea's (1996) beautiful, outraged text on the discarded. He demands of us, it seems to me, that we see in the people who live in the Tiajuana garbage dump about which he writes – literalizations of human waste, living in waste, making themselves from waste, burying children in shallow graves in the waste, quickly forgotten bodies which float up in floods, along with the other waste – the account we must make of the astounding vulnerability of the human person, and somehow find a way to offer ourselves up as such.

In a sense, vast parts of ourselves have become waste in that they need not be practiced or encountered in the regime of global capital: they are superfluous. We might think of these parts of ourselves as those capable of love (agape, charity), of what Terry Eagleton calls "imaginative sympathy" (Eagleton 2003: 133), those parts most linked to the radical possibilities of mimesis. And it is to these parts of ourselves that we might best attend, recover, call back – even as the stages for our corporate performances, and those of our children, proliferate. There are many other things those of us wishing to resist globalizing capital will find we must attend to as well. Attend we must, and attend we will.

I offer this book in that spirit.

Notes

Introduction

1 See for an excellent survey of the term Marvin Carlson's (1996) book, *Performance: A Critical Introduction*.

2 "Perfume" is a word of McKenzie's (2001), used to denote the potential for an inner disintegration of the performance stratum.

I On the move at Niketown and Ralph Lauren

1 Hardt and Negri argue that biopolitical power, which we cooperatively produce through shared networks, creates in us a "productive capacity" that is in excess of the value that capital can harvest from our immaterial labor. See, for instance, Hardt and Negri 2000: 213 or Hardt and Negri 2004: 146. I use the term "productive capacity" here in a more negative sense, as it strikes me as a precise description of what we bring to these shopping environments, precisely the means by which the brand seeds are sown.

2 Hardt and Negri (2000) stress affect as one of the most important products of immaterial labor, and they also identify affectual labor as being a key form of immaterial labor. However, when they use affect they mean it in the conventional way as referring to feelings and emotions.

3 I'm borrowing Karl Marx's much cited and scrutinized example of the table here. See Marx (1967. 71).

4 See http://www.thecityreview.com/ues/madison/lauren.html

5 The deterritorialization wrought by capital is not new. After all, one of the signs of early modern capitalism was the movement away from the market at the geographical center of a village or town where transactions occurred between face to face producers, and to the abstracted circulation of goods in the money form and via middlemen who traveled from place to place. Enclosures of public lands sent huge numbers of the newly landless to be migrant populations of wage-laborers, unsettled from their agricultural identities and life traditions. See, for instance, Fumerton (2000: 206–222) or Agnew (1986: 27–56). Our current situation, though, marks a specifically postindustrial mode

of production, or what Hardt and Negri (2000: 289–90) call the passage
from the Fordist to the Toyotist model.

6   Hardt and Negri (2000: 361–4), more optimistically, conjecture that
migration and exodus and nomadism are a radical potential inherent
in the "multitude" that Empire brings into being.

2 Robots, gods and greed

1   For a fuller discussion of the really made up see Chapter 1. For a quick
overview of the concept here, I say in that chapter:

> Mimesis is a capacity that allows us to travel a spectrum along
> which we encounter, or live, the truth of the make-believe. We
> bring invention into facticity, and vice versa. This means that I
> can live the made up . . . as if it were real. The invented is not
> *just* the made up. It's the "really made up," implying that the made
> up takes on, in our mimetic bodies, the qualities of the real, even
> as it's simultaneously imaginary.

2   For more on the "anti-theatrical prejudice" see Barish (1981).

3   For details on Roman culture and performance see Sennet (1996:
87–101).

4   Here I am thinking especially of the tours of big Broadway hits, and
of the huge hit shows that are finding a permanent home in Las Vegas
itself.

5   I borrow phrasing here, though not conceptual focus, from Derrida's
(1994) "What is Ideology?"

3 *The Lion King*, mimesis, and Disney's magical capitalism

1   See Chapter 2 for a similarly paradoxical relation, at Niketown and
Ralph Lauren, between the promise of the commodity to release people
from the constraints of a market-driven life, and the fact that it is
commodity culture that is creating those constraints in the first place.

2   Disney was a pioneer in conceiving of the store as a stage, and its
employees actors or cast members. This idea is now central to entertainment retail, and much elaborated on by marketing gurus like Pine
and Gilmore. No company, though, has taken the idea to such an
extreme, as we'll see later in the chapter – for Disney, it is essential to
its construction of "magic."

3   I am using quotation marks around the word "primitive" when the
way it is used derives from the imperialist, colonialist and racist discourse
of primitivism, and I am dropping those quotation marks when I use
the word in association with its recovery as a kind of radical difference.

4   Although as I finish this chapter the store has closed, I'll make my
account in the present tense. The show *is* still running and I don't wish
to discuss it in the past tense to be consistent with the store's status.

5   Joseph Roach also discusses the costuming of slaves (see Roach 1996:
212).

4 Making Americans

1 Mini-mags are miniature magazines which come as accessories to the dolls but which contain real information to be read by the real girl.

2 When McKenzie (2001) identifies performance as a new paradigm that shifts the management of subjectivity away from the disciplinary model, he is close to Hardt and Negri's similar identification of a shift from a disciplinary society to "the society of control" (Hardt and Negri 2000: 24 and 329). In my view, however, McKenzie is providing an indispensable theory of a *specific* procedure through which the society of control operates that is lacking in Hardt and Negri.

3 A third store opens in Los Angeles in April 2006.

4 In the video *Felicity's Elegant Tea Party*, the girls visiting Williamsburg are admonished to adopt this secret code with their own mothers and the video ends with slow motion shots of mother's and girl's hands squeezing three times for "I love you," and four times for "I love you too."

5 Although I focus in the chapter on the American Girl Doll Collection, that series of dolls representing the historical characters, there is also a line of dolls that are not historical, and are meant to be dressed in contemporary clothes. They come in three skin shades and many combinations of eye and hair color and hair texture, so that girls can choose one that looks most like her. There are also special limited edition dolls that, like the historical dolls, come with a full array of defining traits and values, and multiple wardrobes for expressing different moods and activities. The boutique sells matching outfits for human girls.

6 Several girls I saw were wearing pink, white and black outfits, clearly deliberately chosen to match the café where they knew they'd be eating. The daisy hair ties they left with were then the *perfect* accessory.

7 The daisy growing from the flowerpot – like the daisy hair elastic that was the napkin holder – is a keepsake. Even the symbolism of these objects underscores the messages that permeate the environment. The daisy dessert presentation seems to be reinforcing the image, through that simple, American flower of growth. The daisy is like the American Girl, grown from American soil, cultivated by America history.

8 The American Girl Doll phenomenon could be the basis for a study in its own right of the intersections of gender and the emerging imperial landscape of corporate power. The word pleasant is key. Elinor Fuchs, reading this chapter, quipped about Pleasant Rowland, "Did she get her name from central casting, or a (literal) Nomenklatura in some missile-proof shelter under the Pentagon?" Interestingly, the American Girl Company is, in the fall and winter of 2005, undergoing sharp criticism for its fundraising (by selling bracelets) for an organization called Girls Inc. This charity serves young girls of color, most of whom live with single mothers with incomes of less than $20,000. Its goals are admirable as listed on a donation solicitation letter: to teach girls to "resist gender stereotypes," to "express themselves with originality," to accept their bodies and to prepare for economic

independence. The Pro-Life Action League in Chicago has organized protests and boycotts of American Girl because they claim that Girls Inc. promotes lesbianism and abortion. The American Girl alliance with Girls Inc. comes on the heels of criticism of American Girls from the Chicago Latino community because the storyline of one of the newer dolls, Marisol, is that she moved from her dangerous inner city Latino neighborhood to the safer suburbs. One could imagine that the support of Girls Inc. is, therefore, a public relations clean-up. Even if it is not, it's important to distrust such corporate moves, to see how American Girl Doll rolls through, absorbs, and ultimately reappears a kind of Second Wave feminism, shaping it through the pleasant performances of girls who hope to be American Girls.

9 The American Girl Clubs are almost surely modeled on the Mickey Mouse Clubs that were, in the 1930s, the founding moment of product tie-ins or "synergy."

10 It's unclear whether this is one of Bush's malapropisms – does he mean reverence?

11 According to James Mann, this nomenclature was coined by Condoleezza Rice after the Roman god Vulcan, "who forged armor and weaponry for the gods and heroes of the ancient world" (http://www.interventionmag.com/cms.modules.php?op=modload&name=News&file=article&sid=1054). The group known as the Vulcans are the substructure of power for which Bush is the figurehead. The following passage indicates the longevity of this substructure and the way that it underlies, as the real source of power, consecutive administrations, working a transition whereby American sovereignty is repositioned within imperial formations of power:

> When George W. Bush campaigned for the White House, he was such a novice in foreign policy that he couldn't name the president of Pakistan. But he was advised by a group that called themselves the Vulcans – a group of men and one woman with long and shared experience in government, dating back to the Nixon, Ford, Reagan, and the first Bush administration. After returning to power in 2001, the Vulcans – including Dick Cheney, Donald Rumsfeld, Colin Powell, Paul Wolfowitz, Richard Armitage, and Condoleezza Rice – were widely expected to restore U.S. foreign policy to what it had been in past Republican administrations. Instead, they put America on an entirely new course, adopting a far-reaching set of ideas and policies that changed the world and America's role in it.
> (http://www.penguin.ca/nf/Book/BookDisplay/0,,0_0670032999,00.html)

12 Although I quote President Bush extensively throughout the chapter, it is important to stress again the longevity of the emerging structures of imperial power. These structures will ensure that, long after Bush is out of power, these kinds of discourses informing "the war on terror," though sure to mutate as needed, will continue.

References

Agnew, J. C. (1986) *Worlds Apart: The Market and the Theatre in Anglo-American Thought, 1550–1750*, New York and Cambridge: Cambridge University Press.

http://www.albertarose.org/Remember/pentagon.htm (accessed 28 June 2005).

Amariglio, J. and Callari, A. (1993) "Marxian Value Theory and the Problem of the Subject: The Role of Commodity Fetishism," in E. Apter and W. Pietz (eds) *Fetishism as Cultural Discourse*, Ithaca, NY and London: Cornell University Press.

http://www.americanparknetwork.com/parkinfo/cw/activities/kidspage. html (accessed 6 June 2005).

Appadurai, A. (1990) *Modernity at Large: Cultural Dimensions of Globalization*, Minneapolis, MN and London: University of Minneapolis Press.

Archer, I. W. (2000) "Material Londoners?," in L. C. Orlin (ed.) *Material London, ca. 1600*, Philadelphia, PA: University of Pennsylvania Press.

http://archives.cnn.com/2001/US/09/16/gen.bush.terrorism/ (accessed 18 January 2005).

Auslander, P. (1999) *Liveness: Performance in a Mediatized Culture*, New York and London: Routledge.

Backscheider, P. R. (1993) *Spectacular Politics: Theatrical Power and Mass Culture in Early Modern England*, Baltimore, MD and London: Johns Hopkins University Press.

Badiou, A. (2003) *Saint Paul: The Foundation of Universalism*, trans. R. Brassier, Stanford, CA: Stanford University Press.

Barish, J. (1981) *The Anti-Theatrical Prejudice*, Berkeley, CA, Los Angeles and London: University of California Press.

Baudrillard, J. (1981) *For a Critique of the Political Economy of the Sign*, trans. Charles Levin, St. Louis, MO: Telos Press.

Bauman, Z. (2004) *Wasted Lives: Modernity and its Outcasts*, Cambridge: Polity.

Benjamin, W. (1968) "The Work of Art in the Age of Mechanical Reproduction," in *Illuminations: Essays and Reflections*, H. Arendt (edited and with introduction by), trans. H. Zohn, New York: Schocken.

—— (1978) "On the Mimetic Faculty," in *Reflections: Essays, Aphorisms, Autobiographical Writings*, P. Demetz (edited and with introduction by), trans. E. Jephcott, New York and London: Harper Brace Jovanovich.

—— (1999) *The Arcades Project*, trans. H. Eiland and K. McLaughlin, Cambridge, MA and London: Belknap Press of Harvard University Press.

Berenson, A. (2004) "The Wonderful World of (Roy) Disney," *The New York Times*, 15 February, sec. 3, p. 6.

http://www.bloomberg.com/apps/news?pid=10000087&sid=a8ySWVU Akf4U&refer=top_world_news (accessed 18 January 2005).

Bourdieu, P. (1984) *Distinction: A Social Critique of the Judgement of Taste*, trans. R. Nice, Cambridge, MA: Harvard University Press.

—— (2000) *Pascalian Meditations*, trans. R. Nice, Stanford, CA: Stanford University Press.

Brantley, B. (1997) "Cub Comes of Age: A Twice-Told Cosmic Tale," *The New York Times*, 14 November, B1.

Bruster, D. (1992) *Drama and the Market in the Age of Shakespeare*, Cambridge: Cambridge University Press.

Buck-Morss, S. (1995) *The Dialectics of Seeing: Walter Benjamin and the Arcades Project*, Cambridge, MA and London: MIT Press.

Butler, J. (2004) *Precarious Life: The Powers of Mourning and Violence*, London and New York: Verso.

Carlson, M. (1996) *Performance: A Critical Introduction*, London and New York: Routledge.

Christian, L. G. (1987) *Theatrum Mundi: The History of an Idea*, New York and London: Garland.

Chung, C. J., Inaba, J., Koolhaas, R. and Leong Sze, T. (eds) (2001) *Harvard Design School Guide to Shopping*, Cologne: Taschen.

http://www.dannhazel.com/Gay%20disney%20Guide%20Sample%20 Chapter.htm (accessed 2 March 2004).

deCordova, R. (1994) "The Mickey in Macy's Window: Childhood, Consumerism, and Disney Animation," in E. Smoodin (ed.) *Disney Discourse: Producing the Magic Kingdom*, New York and London: Routledge.

Derrida, J. (1994) "What is Ideology?," in *Specters of Marx: The State of the Debt, the Work of Mourning, and the New International*, trans. P. Kamuf, New York and London: Routledge.

Diamond, E. (1997) *Unmaking Mimesis*, London and New York: Routledge.

Dorris, V. K. (1997) "NikeTown New York City," *Architectural Record*, 185 (March): 100–3.

Eagleton, T. (2003) *After Theory*, New York: Basic Books.

http://www.forbes.com/business/newswire/2004/02/11rtr1257574.html (accessed 18 February 2004).

http://www.fortune.com/fortune/fsb/specials/innovators/Rowland.html (accessed 17 May 2004).

Foster, H. (1985) *Recodings: Art, Spectacle, Cultural Politics*, Seattle, WA: Bay Press.

Foucault, M. (1979) *Discipline and Punish: The Birth of the Prison*, New York: Vintage.

Fuchs, E. (1996) *The Death of Character: Perspectives on Theater after Modernism*, Bloomington and Indianapolis, IN: Indiana University Press.

Fumerton, P. (2000) "London's Vagrant Economy: Making Space for 'Low' Subjectivity," in L. C. Orlin (ed.) *Material London, ca. 1600*, Philadelphia, PA: University of Pennsylvania Press.

Gaines, J. (1990) "Costume and Narrative: How Dress Tells the Woman's Story," in J. Gaines and C. Herzog (eds) *Fabrications: Costume and the Female Body*, New York and London: Routledge.

http://www.georgebush.com/News/Read.aspx?ID=2955 (accessed 21 July 2004).

Gobe, M. (2001) *Emotional Branding: The New Paradigm for Connecting Brands to People*, New York: Allworth Press.

Goldman, R. and Papson, S. (1996) *Sign Wars: The Cluttered Landscape of Advertising*, New York and London: Guilford Press.

Hardt, M. and Negri, A. (2000) *Empire*, Cambridge, MA and London: Harvard University Press.

—— (2004) *Multitude: War and Democracy in the Age of Empire*, New York: Penguin Press.

Hess, A. (1993) *Viva Las Vegas: After Hours Architecture*, San Francisco, CA: Chronicle Books.

http://www.history.org/Almanack/life/family/esay.cfm#becoming (accessed 25 June 2004).

http://www.history.org/foundation/journal/spring03/president.cfm (accessed 25 June 2004).

http://www.history.org/history/teaching/briggs.cfm (accessed 16 July 2004).

http://www.history.org/history.teaching/colxmas.cfm (accessed 25 June 2004).

Horkheimer, M. and Adorno, T. W. (1972) *Dialectic of Enlightenment*, New York: Continuum.

Huxtable, A. L. (1997) "Living with the Fake and Liking It," *The New York Times*, 30 March, sec. 2.

http://www.interventionmag.com/cms.modules.php?op=modload&name=News&file=article&sid=1054 (accessed 8 June 2005).

Johnson, W. (1999) *Soul by Soul: Life Inside the Antebellum Slave Market*, Cambridge, MA and London: Harvard University Press.

Jones, A. R. and Stallybrass, P. (2000) *Renaissance Clothing and the Materials of Memory*, Cambridge: Cambridge University Press.

Jonson, B. (1979) *The Alchemist*, in R. M. Adams (ed.) *Ben Jonson's Plays and Masques*, New York and London: W. W. Norton.

Kaplan, J. H. and Stowell, S. (1994) *Theatre and Fashion: Oscar Wilde to the Suffragettes*, Cambridge: Cambridge University Press.

Leach, W. (1993) *Land of Desire: Merchants, Power, and the Rise of a New American Culture*, New York: Vintage.

Lindström, M. (2003) *BRANDchild: Remarkable Insights into the Minds of Today's Global Kids and their Relationships with Brands*, London and Sterling, VA: Kogan Page.

McKenzie, J. (2001) *Perform or Else: From Discipline to Performance*, London and New York: Routledge.

Maddox, D. (1984) *Semiotics of Deceit: the Pathelin Era; with a new English Prose Translation of Maistre Pierre Pathelin by Alan E. Knight*, Lewisburg, PA: Bucknell University Press.

Marx, K. (1967) *Capital: A Critique of Political Economy, Vol. I: The Process of Capitalist Production*, trans. S. Moore and E. Aveling, New York: International Publishers.

Massumi, B. (2002) *Parables for the Virtual: Movement, Affect, Sensation*, Durham, NC and London: Duke University Press.

Mizejewski, L. (1999) *Ziegfeld Girl: Image and Icon in Culture and Cinema*, Durham, NC and London: Duke University Press.

Moskin, J. (2004) "It's the Hottest Place in Town, and Dolls Eat Free," *The New York Times*, 16 May, p. 1.

Peck, J. (1997) "Anne Oldfield's Lady Townly: Consumption, Credit, and the Whig Hegemony of the 1720s," *Theatre Journal*, 49(4): 397–416.

http://www.penguin.ca/nf/Book/BookDisplay/0,,0_0670032999,00.html (accessed 8 June 2005).

Pietz, W. (1993) "Fetishism and Materialism: The Limits of Theory in Marx," in E. Apter and W. Pietz (eds) *Fetishism as Cultural Discourse*, Ithaca, NY and London: Cornell University Press.

http://pressroom.hallmark.com/American_girl_holiday03.html (accessed 20 June 2004).

http://www.pruiksma.com/A%20NOT%20So%20Silly%20Symphony.html (accessed 2 March 2004).

Quart, A. (2003) *Branded: The Buying and Selling of Teenagers*, Cambridge: Perseus.

Riewoldt, H. V. (2002) *Brandscaping: Worlds of Experience in Retail Design*, Basel: Birkhäuser; London: Momenta.

Roach, J. (1996) *Cities of the Dead: Circum-Atlantic Performance*, New York: Columbia University Press.

http://savedisney.com/news/essays/rd020904.1.asp (accessed 18 February 2004).

Schickel, R. (1997) *The Disney Version: The Life, Times, Art and Commerce of Walt Disney*, Chicago: Elephant Paperbacks.

Sennet, R. (1996) *Flesh and Stone: The Body and the City in Western Civilization*, New York and London: Norton.

Seremetakis, C. N. (1994) "The Memory of the Senses, Part I: Marks of the Transitory," in C. N. Seremetakis (ed.) *The Senses Still: Perception and Memory as Material Culture in Modernity*, Chicago: University of Chicago Press.

Shaw, J. (1988) *Changes for Kirsten: A Winter Story*, Madison, WI: Pleasant Company.

http://www.showmenews.com/2004/Oct/20041023News026.asp (accessed 20 January 2005).

Siegel, D., Coffey, T. J. and Livingston, G. (2001) *The Great Tween Buying Machine: Marketing to Today's Tweens*, Ithaca, NY: Paramount Market.

Siegel, R. (2000) *All Things Considered*, Transcript, National Public Radio, 2 November.

Taussig, M. (1993) *Mimesis and Alterity: A Particular History of the Senses*, London and New York: Routledge.

http://www.thecityreview.com/ues/madison/lauren.html (accessed 10 January 2006).

The Project on Disney (1995) "Working at the Rat," in *Inside the Mouse: Work and Play at Disney World*, Durham, NC and London: Duke University Press.

Troy, N. J. (2001) "The Theatre of Fashion: Staging Haute Couture in Early 20th Century France," *Theatre Journal*, 53(1): 1–32.

Turner, J. G. (1995) "The New Exchange: Female Entrepreneurs," in A. Bermingham and J. Brewer (eds) *The Consumption of Culture 1600–1800*, London and New York: Routledge.

Urrea, L. A. (1996) *By the Lake of Sleeping Children: The Secret Life of the Mexican Border*, New York and London: Anchor Books Doubleday.

http://www.usembassy.org.uk/bush299.html (accessed 28 June 2005).

Venturi, R., Brown, D. S. and Izenour, S. (1972) *Learning from Las Vegas*, Cambridge, MA: MIT Press.

Wallace, M. (1996) *Mickey Mouse History and Other Essays on American Memory*, Philadelphia, PA: Temple University Press.

http://washingtontimes.com/national/20040623–124644–1098r.htm (accessed 29 June 2005).

http://www.whitehouse.gov/news/releases/2001/09/20010925–5.html (accessed 20 January 2005).

http://www.whitehouse.gov/news/releases/2001/10/20011016–4.html (accessed 19 January 2005).

http://www.whitehouse.gov/news/releases/2001/11/20011108–13.html (accessed 17 December 2004).

http://www.whitehouse.gov/news/releases/2004/12/20041217–1.html1 (accessed 17 December 2004).

Willis, S. (1991) *A Primer for Daily Life*, London and New York: Routledge.

Winer, L. (1997) "Lion King Leads a Magical, Rich Jungle Parade", *The New York Times*, 17 November, B3.

Index

power 48, 49, 50, 105, 154–5;
biopolitical 11–12; disciplinary
104; of performance 145, 147
primitive fetish 84–5, 88–9
the primitive: commodification of
86, 88–9; mimesis and 84–6
production, decentralized 39–40
productive capacity 15–21, 26, 27,
39; affect as 21–4; imagination
as 48–9
The Project on Disney 81–3
Pruiksma, D. 92, 93

Quart, A. 120

race 146
Ralph Lauren 15, 27–8, 30–9
real fake 47
really made up 2, 6, 19–20, 37, 39
Reinwoldt, Otto 14
religious fetishism 85
Renaissance, and theatrum mundi
53, 54–5, 56, 59
representation 5–6
resistance 10
Rhinelander, Philip Jacob 31
Rhinelander-Waldo, Gertrude 31
Rice, Condoleeza 145, 160 n.11
Riewoldt, H. V. 17–18, 20
Roach, J. 57
robotic performance 57–9, 61–2,
64, 80
Rockefeller family 99, 100
Roman culture 57–8
Rowland, Pleasant 96–7, 98, 99,
100, 106, 119

Sarno, Jay 46
Schickel, R. 68, 71
self/selves 7, 8
senses 120–1
September 11 2001 102
Shaw, J. 108
Siegel, Robert 2–3, 120
Simonson, Lee 32
slaves/slavery 89–91, 142–3
society: of control 11, 12, 40, 41,
49, 159 n.2; disciplinary 11, 41,
104, 159 n.2
Spinelli (actress) 117

Stallybrass, P. 116
Stoics 53–4
Stowell, S. 117
structuration 105, 108, 110
subjectivity 7, 79, 80; and the
commodity 73–8, 89–91;
production of 40–1
sumptuary laws 115
surrogation 50, 57–63

Tamara 59
Taussig, M. 2, 16–17, 19, 20, 22,
67, 68, 84, 85, 89
Taymor, J. 86–7
technological performance 104,
146, 147
terrorists/terrorism 149, 150–1
Tertullian 54
theatre 5–6, 8, 115–18, 122
theatrum mundi 49–50, 53–63, 65
Time magazine 68
Tony and Tina's Wedding 59–60
Troy, N. 117
Turner, J. G. 115
2gether 2–3

Urban, Joseph 32
Urrea, Luis Alberto 156
use-value 7, 24–7, 39, 63

values, American 99, 101, 102–3
Venturi, R. 45, 46
visibility 111–12
Vives, J.-L. 55
Vulcans 145, 160 n.11

Wallace, M. 100, 126, 143
Wanamakers 32
Warner Brothers store 78–9
wealth, inherited 34–5
Webster, John 8
Wexler, Barrie 59
Wheeler, John 9
Willis, Susan 26
Winer, L. 87
Wolfowitz, Paul 145, 160 n.11
women, exchange 115
women's bodies 113–18

Ziegfeld Follies 117, 118

Related titles from Routledge

Brands

Marcel Danesi

Marcel Danesi's outstanding introduction provides a clear guide to brands and brand identity, outlining their historical origins and their increasing centrality in contemporary consumer culture. He introduces:

- the origins of brands
- naming and brand image
- how semiotic theory can be used to analyze brand image
- brands and consumer culture
- advertising campaigns
- brands in the global village
- the anti-brand movement.

Danesi shows how consumer products such as cars, perfume and even websites are sold to us through the creation of powerful brand images, and analyzes the advertising campaigns developed to promote brands such as Coca-Cola, McDonalds, Absolut Vodka, Apple, Gucci and Chanel. He also discusses the rise of the anti-brand movement, and its challenges to the dominance of global brands such as Gap and Nike.

Including an annotated guide to further reading, details of useful websites and a comprehensive bibliography, Danesi's book is an important contribution to the field of marketing and communications.

ISBN 10: 0–415–27997–6 (hbk)
ISBN 10: 0–415–27998–4 (pbk)
ISBN 13: 978–0–415–27997–0 (hbk)
ISBN 13: 978–0–415–27998–7 (pbk)

Available at all good bookshops
For ordering and further information please visit:
www.routledge.com

Related titles from Routledge

Electoral Guerrilla Theatre: Radical Ridicule and Social Movements

L.M. Bogad

'*Electoral Guerrilla Theatre* deals a refreshing 'wild-card in the repertoire of resistance' – libertarian legislative theatre for the MTV, hard-wired, chilled-out, anti-globalisation generation.'

Baz Kershaw, *University of Bristol*

'As a guide to both theory and action, it is insightful, entertaining and indispensable.'

Andrew Boyd, *Billionaires for Bush*

'Beautifully contextualized within social movement theory, this book enlivens the debate about performative interventions into power.'

Jan Cohen Cruz, *New York University*

Across the globe, in liberal democracies where the right to vote is framed as both civil right and civic duty, disillusioned creative activists run for public office on ironic and outrageous platforms. With little intention of winning in the conventional sense, they use drag, camp and stand-up comedy to undermine the legitimacy of their opponents and call into question the electoral system itself.

Drawing on extensive archival and ethnographic research, L.M. Bogad explores the recent phenomenon of satirical election campaigns, asking:

- What is their purpose?
- What theatrical devices and aesthetic sensibilities do electoral guerrillas draw on for their satire?
- How do parodies and the 'respectable' political performances they mock interact? How can this tactic backfire?

Electoral Guerrilla Theatre offers an entertaining and enlightening read for students working across a variety of disciplines, including performance studies, social science, cultural studies and politics.

ISBN 10: 0–415–33224–9 (hbk)
ISBN 10: 0–415–33225–7 (pbk)
ISBN 13: 978–0–415–33224–8 (hbk)
ISBN 13: 978–0–415–33225–5 (pbk)

Available at all good bookshops
For ordering and further information please visit:
www.routledge.com

Related titles from Routledge

Perform or Else:
From Discipline to
Performance

Jon McKenzie

'Incredibly smart, provocative, and important.'
  – Janelle Reinelt, *University of California, Davis*
'Wholly original, extremely valuable'
  – Philip Auslander, *Georgia Institute of Technology*

'Performance' has become one of the key terms for the new century. But what do we mean by 'performance'? In today's world it can refer to experimental art; productivity in the workplace; and technological and scientific breakthroughs. Do these disparate fields bear any conceptual relation to each other?

In *Perform or Else*, Jon McKenzie asserts that there is an uncanny relationship between cultural, organisational, and technological performance. In this theoretical tour de force McKenzie demonstrates brilliantly that all three paradigms operate together to create powerful and contradictory pressures to 'perform . . . or else'.

This is an urgent and important intervention in contemporary critical thinking. It will profoundly shape our understanding of twenty-first-century structures of power and knowledge.

ISBN 10: 0–415–24768–3 (hbk)
ISBN 10: 0–415–24769–1 (pbk)
ISBN 13: 978–0–415–24768–9 (hbk)
ISBN 13: 978–0–415–24769–6 (pbk)

Available at all good bookshops
For ordering and further information please visit:
www.routledge.com

eBooks – at www.eBookstore.tandf.co.uk

A library at your fingertips!

eBooks are electronic versions of printed books. You can store them on your PC/laptop or browse them online.

They have advantages for anyone needing rapid access to a wide variety of published, copyright information.

eBooks can help your research by enabling you to bookmark chapters, annotate text and use instant searches to find specific words or phrases. Several eBook files would fit on even a small laptop or PDA.

NEW: Save money by eSubscribing: cheap, online access to any eBook for as long as you need it.

Annual subscription packages

We now offer special low-cost bulk subscriptions to packages of eBooks in certain subject areas. These are available to libraries or to individuals.

For more information please contact webmaster.ebooks@tandf.co.uk

We're continually developing the eBook concept, so keep up to date by visiting the website.

www.eBookstore.tandf.co.uk